SECOND LIVES

Becoming a

Desktop
Publisher

S0-EBU-576

Also by Bill Harris

Second Lives: Becoming a Consultant
Second Lives: Becoming a Freelance Writer

Becoming a
Desktop
Publisher

BILL HARRIS

Introduction by Charles L. Sodikoff, Ph.D.

St. Martin's Griffin ⚐ New York

Library of Congress Cataloging-in-Publication Data

Harris, Bill.
    Second lives : becoming a desktop publisher / Bill Harris.—1st St. Martin's Griffin ed.
      p.   cm.
    ISBN 0-312-20003-X
    1. Desktop publishing industry—United States—Management. I. Title.
Z244.645.U6H37   1999
686.2'2544536'068—dc21   99-15140
                                    CIP

First St. Martin's Griffin Edition: August 1999

10 9 8 7 6 5 4 3 2 1

Contents

INTRODUCTION

Starting over? What does that mean to you? To some it means opportunity, challenge, and growth. To others it means danger and defeat. To everyone it means *change*.

Change is defining the course of America today. Millions of us who have spent the first part of our working lives employed by someone else are now—either unwillingly or by our own initiative—starting over. The options are clear: find another job in your current trade, find a job in a new trade, retire (if you can afford it), or work for yourself.

Second Lives is a guidebook for those who are considering using the experience and skills acquired working for someone else to go into business for themselves.

Going into business is like learning to ride a bike. Remember that first try? Someone held the bike and ran alongside. You pumped your legs as hard as you could, wobbling wildly as you tried to keep the front wheel straight. Then suddenly you were on your own, but you probably didn't get very far. Maybe you scraped your knees when you fell.

After that there were some more bumpy rides, falls, and scrapes, but eventually the ride smoothed out and a whole new world opened up. Our lives changed. We had more independence. We traveled to new places and did new things. We kept up with some of our friends and left others in the dust.

That's exactly what starting a new business is like.

Second Lives is the guiding hand on the back of your bicycle. It will help you make the decision as to whether or not to go off on your own, identify the type of business you ought to pursue, and give you the support to launch your business successfully.

Starting your own business may be the most exciting but hair-raising adventure you ever take. I know, not only because I have counseled many people who have tried it, but also because I have done it myself. At age forty-eight, I decided to open my own consulting practice after years and years of working for someone else. The trip has been exhilarating and my second life has been the happiest of my entire career. Sure, there have been scary periods and times when I wasn't so certain I would succeed, but with a strong motivation, the proper skills, and the flexibility to adapt to the ever-changing needs of my business, I am well on my way.

I hope this book helps you make the right decision for yourself. If you do choose to go out on your own, put on your helmet and be prepared for the most exciting ride of your life.

—Charles L. Sodikoff, Ph.D.

CHAPTER ONE

A World of Your Own

At one time or another, just about everyone has had the dream of being self-employed. Right now, that may be your dream, and if the job description that goes with it is "desktop publisher," you couldn't have picked a better time. The demand for the services of desktop publishers has been growing since graphic artists and word processors began working with personal computers in the mid-1970s. In fact, as computers get faster and software more versatile, many desktop publishers are convinced they haven't scratched the surface, not only of what they're able to accomplish, but of their ever-growing list of potential clients in the world around them.

The decision of whether or not to go into business for yourself is one of the most important you'll ever face and will take a great deal of soul searching. Starting your own business takes a lot of courage. One of the biggest stumbling blocks you may be facing

I thought about starting my own business for fifteen years before I actually did it. I had a good job, and I didn't want to give up that steady paycheck. But now I'm sorry I didn't do it a lot sooner.

—Shawn Teets, Wordwise, Indianapolis, IN

> Although I work extremely long hours now that I'm on my own, I love my boss! And I make at least three times what I did as an employee.
>
> —Cindy Dyer, Dyer Designs, Alexandria, VA

is fear of change. Most people find change frightening, but it may not be unfamiliar territory. Chances are you're not doing your job in the same way as you did five or ten years ago, and you've been dealing with change for longer than you might think. Back in your father's day, holding a job for twenty or thirty years often added up to one year's experience twenty or thirty times. But experience is something quite different in today's world. You may be surprised to find that change is already a large part of your life.

Another key consideration is the question of security. There are no guaranteed weekly paychecks or health benefits when you're on your own. But keep in mind that security also has a new meaning today. Not too many years ago, people expected to retire from the same job they started out with, whether they liked it or not. But companies have changed and so have people. Attitudes also have undergone changes. Nobody expects a job to last a lifetime anymore. The silver lining in all this is that we're all freer than we've ever been to try something new and change our lives. There may never be a better time to put yourself in control of your own destiny.

YOU'RE NOT ALONE

Being in charge of your own life is at the heart of the American dream. It's the same promise that brought our ancestors here; it's what built the country, and it is what still drives millions of Americans.

> I was typing medical transcriptions for a living, and I hated it.
> Now that I'm in business for myself, I'm making a better living,
> and I'm getting more satisfaction out of my life.
>   Susan Abbott, Abbott & Abbott, St. Paul, MN

According to a 1997 survey by the Entrepreneurial Research Consortium, as many as 4 percent of American adults are in the process of starting up more than three million small businesses. The survey also revealed that one out of every three U.S. households—thirty-five million of them—includes someone who has followed the dream of going into business for himself or herself at one time or another. It's happening all around you. Old people, young people, men and women walking away from unsatisfying nine-to-five jobs, time-wasting commutes, office politics, and unappreciative bosses.

Many of us have had a boss who was either unfair, unyielding, incompetent, insensitive, mean-spirited, double-dealing, or all of the above. That's no fun, and one of the reasons why you may have bought this book is because you don't want to spend the rest of your life working for people who sometimes seem to go out of their way to make life difficult.

Going into business for yourself gives you a chance to use the skills you've developed working for someone else to create a whole new life—only this time it can be tailored specifically for you, with more freedom, interest, and satisfaction.

Of course, it's pretty easy to talk yourself into staying put. You might tell yourself that striking out on your own isn't a realistic thing to do. But consider one of the joyous realities of modern life: we're all probably going to live to celebrate our seventy-fifth birthdays, and most likely quite a few after that. Do you really want the second half of your life to be a carbon copy of the first? These days, there are so many different options and opportuni-

> I was laid off from my job with a printing company, and went to work for a desktop publisher for less money to get the experience. Then one day I said, "Boy! I could be doing this for myself."
>
> —Kevin Edwards, Duluth, GA

ties out there—especially in the expanding world of desktop publishing.

Consider what's happening in corporate America. Downsizing leaves hundreds out of work, Wall Street cheers, and the victims have anxiety attacks. The gurus of big business preach that getting rid of deadwood cuts a company's costs, the survivors work a bit harder, and stock prices go up. But there is only so much extra work a company can squeeze from its people, and its commitment to stay lean and mean usually means it can't hire new employees either.

These days it's considered good business for companies to "go outside" and hire independent contractors to get the work done. By and large, that represents a huge opportunity for graphic artists and word processors and is good news for the future of your desktop publishing business. Even companies that have grown rather than downsized are using more outside help now than ever before. It's a very good reason to consider declaring yourself an outsider.

FOLLOW YOUR DREAM

At one time or another, everybody has dreamed of making it big. Some do, and some just make it better. The first step is to get rid of the illusion that we need to play out the hand we've been dealt.

It's never too late to wipe the slate clean and take charge. It's

I read tons and tons of books on computers, and was fascinated with what they could do. Then, two years ago, I made up my own business and people started coming to me—I just love my job.

—Ellen Connor, Connor Custom Creations,
Fayetteville, NC

your life, after all, and there is no reason why it ought to be unsatisfying. If you think your own ideas are better, don't waste them on the suggestion box. Use them for yourself. You never know where they'll take you—until you try.

CHAPTER TWO

What Exactly Is a Desktop Publisher?

Sue Karlin's company, Suka & Friends, is based in a 1,500-square-foot loft in the New York City neighborhood known as SoHo. Her staff of four produces four-color inserts for *The New York Times*, glossy annual reports for nonprofit organizations such as the YMCA and the American Health Association, and collateral material for Fortune 500 companies. In Louisville, Kentucky, Karen Cunningham works in her living room, typing papers for students, and providing transcriptions of medical and legal papers as well as focus group output. She also produces résumés, manuscripts, and how-to employee manuals. And in what spare time she has left, she provides proofreading and editing services.

Both Sue and Karen are desktop publishers. Although Sue's company turns out colorful pieces with print runs in the millions, and Karen usually delivers black-and-white jobs that require less than a dozen copies, each of them is part of a profession with an ancestry as old as the printed word itself.

A NEW FIELD, AN OLD TRADITION

Back before there were media empires, anyone with a pen and access to a printing press was called a publisher, which simply meant someone who made ideas "public" through printed words or drawings. More often than not, that someone took care of every detail from originating the concept to setting type to distributing the printed message to a waiting public.

Now, thanks to desktop computers, history is repeating itself, and the word "publisher" is no longer appropriated solely by the rich and powerful. Like our ancestors in the business of ideas, desktop publishers get involved in every step in the production of a printed page. Today, however, publishers enjoy a powerful partnership—with their computers.

THE DESKTOP PUBLISHER'S LEGACY

In the not-too-distant past, even creating a simple promotional piece was a labor-intensive project. Someone first had to make a comprehensive, detailed layout, called a "comp," showing how illustrations and type would be arranged on a page. Then type styles had to be specified for the copy and sent to a typographer, who typically took all night to set it and pull the proofs. If mistakes were made, they had to be corrected at the type house, where more time was lost before the job could go on to the next step, the creation of a "mechanical," or "pasteup." That painstaking process involved cutting all the elements into small pieces and rubber-cementing them to a sheet of paperboard that would eventually go to a printer for plate making. But, alas, before it went on to the printer, the finished mechanicals, sometimes called "camera-ready art," had to be processed by a production person. It was this person's job to add instructions, traffic the proofs back and forth from the printer, and then make sure the finished job was delivered on time.

At the minimum, not counting the typographer, who took great pleasure from charging extra if the type was needed in a hurry, three people were kept quite busy getting a simple flyer ready to go to the printer. This could easily add up to some twenty-four man-hours, and for a more elaborate brochure, it might have been five or six times as many. When salaries, fringe benefits, and office rent were added together, the cost was prohibitive for most small companies and organizations.

THE DESKTOP PUBLISHER'S ADVANTAGE

Although there are some printers with outdated union agreements who still require the old-style camera-ready art or big investments in old-fashioned equipment those days are just about gone forever.

Desktop publishers are giving individuals, organizations, and companies of every size an advantage they didn't have a few years ago. Thanks to them, clients have access to better design and faster service. And it is now easier for desktop publishers to give those clients exactly what they want, because the computer makes it possible to make changes without starting from scratch.

The growth of desktop publishing is having an effect on nearly everyone's life. We're all getting more newsletters in the mail these days, more flyers slipped under our doors, more magazines to satisfy the most esoteric of interests, and more inserts that make getting bills more interesting (though no less painful!). The desktop computer has made it cheaper and easier to create better custom-designed visuals. And the demand for them is growing, literally day after day.

Clients who remember the painstaking, costly processes of the past know they're getting a bargain when they use the services of a desktop publisher. But, although they save their clients' money, desktop publishers don't lose money doing it. Depending on where they're doing business, even startup operators handling relatively simple jobs can easily earn two hundred fifty dollars to three hundred dollars a day.

Everyone appreciates the time-saving efficiency of today's process. With a computer and the right software, one person does it all: from the designing and the typesetting to the creation of finished art in the form of a simple computer disk. Better still, most desktop publishers then bring the disk to the printer and deliver finished material to their clients. Some even make themselves more indispensable—and add to their income—by providing mailing service, too.

THE VISUAL ARTS

Operators of desktop publishing businesses have another big advantage over their predecessors. Their computers make it easier for them to turn out high-quality work without the long apprenticeships that were once considered indispensable to good design. They have easy access to an almost infinite number of different typefaces, along with graphics, photography, and other elements of design that computer programs allow them to manipulate into something entirely original.

Using these programs, it has become possible for a single person to get the kind of results that once required teams of experts. The computer makes it relatively easy to design business cards, letterheads, advertisements, brochures and flyers and entire direct-mail packages. You can even learn to retouch photographs or produce a book.

With new applications being developed on a near-daily basis, designing by computer isn't just an idea whose time has come, it is an idea with a big future.

WORD PROCESSING SERVICES

Although many desktop publishers have a background in the graphic arts, it isn't the only way to take advantage of the opportunities the computer has opened up. Far from it.

For example, right now, you may be giving serious thought to giving up the nine-to-five rat race and striking out on your own.

Fortunately for you, thousands of people are racing off in the other direction and every one of them needs a résumé to help them get a job. A word processing program makes it simple for you to offer a variety of typestyles and layouts and to produce résumés that are custom-tailored to specific job offerings.

Karen Cunningham says that when she went into business, "I didn't plan to do résumés at all, let alone write them. Now I find I probably do about 30 percent of my business in 'writing' résumés, something I never thought would happen." And, she adds, it's not just a profitable sideline, but "it's part of a potpourri of different types of work, and that tends to break up the monotony of doing any one thing for long."

Even if you've never designed so much as an invitation to a child's birthday party, word processing represents an opportunity to build a solid business. And if the design aspects scare you, don't worry: your computer has a flair for it. By using clip art and stock photography, you can create snappy-looking pages that add a new dimension to nearly any word processing job. And with a good graphics program, you'll find it is easy to create basic graphs and charts to enhance reports, presentations, and technical documents.

NEWSLETTERS: TURNING A HOBBY INTO A BUSINESS

Business newsletters, one niche area alone, is a five-billion-dollar-a-year industry. There are some big players taking the lion's share, of course. But a good percentage of the ten thousand newsletter titles being published today are produced by independent desktop publishers who started out with a couple of articles, a mailing list, and a good word processing program on their home computers. Many of those entrepreneurs came from the business world, and now they're using their experience and contacts in a business of their own. They specialize in offering information a subscriber can't easily find elsewhere, and the more exclusive the information, the higher the subscription price. It can go as high as fifteen hundred dollars a year—per subscriber—for weekly updates on subjects ranging from Internet business strategies to updates on global warming.

If you have a passion that has become an area of expertise, the computer can give you a terrific way to turn your hobby into a business. Anything that interests you probably interests a whole lot of other people, too. If you were to research and publish a newsletter on, say, collecting teddy bears or growing daylilies, it is quite possible you'd become the authority people interested in those things will turn to—not to mention pay—and subscribe to your newsletter. All it takes is knowledge in your field of interest, a dash of enthusiasm, and a desktop computer.

PREPARING MANUSCRIPTS

Among the clients that keep word processing professionals thriving are other professionals in such fields as medicine and education who write lengthy papers but don't usually have the time or talent to get them into publishable form.

Almost every kind of manuscript, from books and screenplays to articles, legal briefs, and scientific papers, needs to be submitted in a format as professional as the content. No publisher wants to read typewritten pages thick with White-Out. In fact, most insist on getting a computer disk along with clean hard copy. And there are doctors, professors, lawyers, writers, and others out there who need to be published but who have been too busy keeping up with their own fields to catch up with the changing capabilities of the computer.

Karen Cunningham has found that typing manuscripts for writers is one of her best profit makers, but she has turned it into an even better one by offering editing services as well. "I just fell into that," she confides. "Lots of people seem to have something to say and want to put it into hard copy. But they often have trouble putting a proper sentence together. That's just fine with me because I can make extra money doing it for them." Her computer also makes it relatively easy for her to create indexes and bibliographies, a valuable service to her writer clients, but equally valuable to her as a source of extra income.

DIRECT MAIL

For a desktop publisher, direct mail is a huge area of opportunity. The computer makes maintaining mailing lists as easy as producing the material that goes out in the mail. You can even buy a postage meter, so you won't have to visit the post office quite so often. While you're there, don't forget to ask about postal permits. For clients who do regular mailings, a permit number on a return card means postage doesn't have to be paid unless the card is actually returned.

There are potential clients for direct mail in almost every kind of small business, from restaurants to retail stores to the various associations right in your own neighborhood. The list goes on to large organizations as well, such as banks, realtors, and car dealerships; even political organizations and health care providers.

Paul Hacker, a desktop publisher in Staten Island, New York, creates newsletters, flyers, and membership mailings for Classical America, an organization of architectural historians. He also takes care of getting his handiwork into the mail. He keeps the organization's mailing lists current, collects members' annual dues, and fulfills mail-order requests for books written by its members. It all began when they hired him to produce simple mailing pieces, but it wasn't long before he convinced them that he could do the other things as well. "Now they call me their business manager," he says. "But my business is still desktop publishing. Keeping track of lists and records is just one more thing my computer can do."

Handling direct mail for smaller clients often requires little more than the creation of simple letters and flyers. They usually use their own lists—customers, prospects, members—but may need someone who can create a database to manage those lists for them. They know they'll save postage if their lists are sorted by zip code, a simple thing for a desktop publisher but too time-consuming for the average small businessperson. Many like the idea of personalizing their letters, another thing you and your computer can easily do.

Big users of direct mail like catalog merchants, magazine publishers, and software developers regard direct mail as a science. They rent huge targeted mailing lists and carefully analyze the responses they get. But even they are turning to desktop publishers for help with the design and production of their mailings, which often include elaborate multicolor brochures, return cards, and flashy inserts. Although direct-mail experts understand how to make their mailings productive, more often than not the experts who actually produce those mailings are desktop publishers.

Tony Fry, who works out of his home in San Rafael, California, has established himself as one of those experts, even though until a few years ago he had never given much thought to direct mail. He was designing brochures and collateral material for insurance companies when he met a copywriter who introduced him to a direct-mail packager. As often happens in the desktop publishing business, his networking created a new niche for him—a second life after nearly thirty years in the design business.

CREATING YOUR OWN OPPORTUNITIES

Desktop publishers can be as creative about what they do as they are in how they do it. No matter what your specialty may be, there are always a host of avenues and new opportunities to explore. For instance, a lot of word processing specialists take advantage of the slow season that sometimes comes around the year-end holidays to pursue a new path. In some cases, they have turned this period into a busy time by producing and mailing letters from Santa Claus, commissioned by eager parents, grand-parents, and others who enjoy making kids happy.

Shelley Newman, who runs an office services/résumé desktop publishing business, and also hosts America Online's "Original Santa Letter Chat," says that in the first year, "profit is usually around $1,000." On a personal note, she adds that, "This year, I hope to reach $4,000, and that will really help fill in for those slow months. It isn't the norm, but I know of one person who sends out thousands of Santa letters and grosses around $60,000." (That's not a bad Christmas bonus!) Ms. Newman adds, "If you do this a number of years and get all that repeat business—and I promise you, people keep coming back—it gets easier and easier to make money."

The computer makes it possible to make personalized Santa letters that include such things as the names of siblings and pets, schools and teachers, and, of course, parents and grandparents—the ones who are going to pay you. It is simply a matter of setting up a standard letter in your word processing program and merg-ing the specifics from a database. Use clip art to create a colorful letterhead and envelope and you're in business (some of Santa's elves also embellish their letters with stickers and stencils, and some enclose small gifts).

Where do you get the business? Ms. Newman says, "I strongly suggest using this as a fund-raiser for charities you feel close to. I use a domestic violence shelter program as my charity, and donate $1 per letter to them. It's a great marketing tool, and it generates a lot of good will." (Not to mention a tax deduction.) In her book, *The Most Comprehensive Santa Letter Package*, she writes, "Contact the public relations department of the charity you have chosen and make them aware of your pending donation. They may want to help distribute flyers or use other forms of publicity to help increase the donated amount." She also promotes the idea on her own, and suggests posting flyers at places where parents and grandparents are likely to turn up. Her most successful location is credit union bulletin boards, but she doesn't neglect places such as fast-food stores and dentists' offices.

And although Santa Claus is seasonal, sending out letters to youngsters isn't. Did you ever meet a child who doesn't like to get mail? The Easter Bunny is an obvious corollary, but every kid has a birthday, and then there's the first day of school, the first lost tooth, the arrival of a new baby. In the world of desktop publishing, the opportunities are as endless as your imagination.

GO FOR IT

Ellen Connor got married right out of high school, had two children but no other career. In hopes of finding a profession, she took a computer course but decided there was no future in it for her. Then she began browsing the Internet, chatted with people online, and read "tons and tons of books." Then, after a year or two of research, she decided that maybe there was a future for her in computers after all. "I made my business up as I went along," she says, "and people just started coming to me. I just instantly fell in love with my job." Today her company, Connor Custom Creations in Fayetteville, North Carolina, produces business cards, letterheads, and brochures for small companies and individuals, as well as newsletters for local organizations.

Six months after Ellen started her business, she had enough work to cover her start-up costs and her expenses, and she is still going strong. And what's on the horizon for this woman who once thought there was no place for her in the world of computers? "I think the biggest opportunity for me right now is in designing Web sites," she predicts. "It's really taking off." She still keeps expanding her regular desktop publishing business, but, as she's discovered, new opportunities keep presenting themselves. And that's one of the things that makes desktop publishing really unique.

CHAPTER THREE

A Day in the Life of a Desktop Publisher

The prospect of not having a boss interrupting you every five minutes may be one of the reasons you're planning to be your own boss one of these days, but don't think there won't be interruptions you didn't plan for, and days without enough hours to get everything done.

No more than there is a typical desktop publisher, there is no such thing as a "typical" day when you become one, except possibly that many of them are long. When you begin working for yourself, your routine will be determined by your own rhythms. Some people find they work best late at night, others believe they do their best work at the crack of dawn. Either way, you won't be living in a nine-to-five world anymore, and although you'll need to be bright-eyed and bushy-tailed for contact with your clients during their regular business day, you will be free to do the work at times when you feel most productive.

However, that doesn't mean you can put off doing the work until you "feel like it." Self-discipline may be the key to success in many small businesses, but it is crucial in desktop publishing. Set up a routine for yourself and work at following it. The nature of the job gives you all the variety you could wish for, but it's best if you come up with a suitable schedule that you don't vary from unless it's unavoidable.

A few desktop publishers interviewed for this book agreed to describe a day selected at random, each in their own way and in their own words. All of them work from home offices, and none has any employees. The days they chose may not be typical of their overall working lives, nor of yours when you go into business for yourself, but together they'll give you some clues about what might lie ahead.

SUSAN ABBOTT—Abbott & Abbott, St. Paul, MN

When her daughter was born five years ago, Susan became a desktop publisher after fifteen years of working as a typist for several different printing companies. Working for herself gives flexibility to her day and more time to share with her daughter. Most of her clients are printing brokers (people who sell printers' services) and small publishers.

8A.M. Made delivery of color maps and floor plans for a real estate presentation.

9A.M. Returned phone calls received while I was out making the delivery. Got ready for my daughter's piano lesson.

10–11A.M. Took my daughter to the piano teacher, did grocery shopping.

11A.M.–1P.M. Returned phone calls received while I was gone. Worked on logo ideas for a new client. Converted files E-mailed from a client into readable format. Fixed my daughter's lunch.

1–2:30P.M. Volunteer day at the kindergarten.

2:30–3:30P.M. Delivered ads I created for a neighborhood newspaper and dropped off a job at the quick printer.

3:30–6P.M. Returned messages; answered phone calls. Did production work on a logo design, and a little bit of accounting, posting payments and credit card statements.

6–6:30P.M. Dinner with family.

6:30–MIDNIGHT Production work: newspaper ads, floor plan insert for a convention directory (an emergency job that came in at 4 P.M.), alterations to a four-color booklet (came in at 10 P.M.). Checked E-mail. Made list of tasks for tomorrow. Shuffled priorities. Sent overnight faxes and packed up newspaper ads for morning delivery.

CINDY DYER—Dyer Designs, Alexandria, VA
After several years as a graphic designer for different companies, Cindy became an independent desktop publisher in 1985. Most of her business is designing newsletters, magazines, books, and annual reports. Her days are typically long, but she says she likes it that way. She recharges her batteries with regular short vacations.

I started working in the studio at 8:30 . . . finished typesetting some small jobs for a local printing shop. (It's low pay per piece, but high volume. Sometimes it's worth it, sometimes not.) Then I faxed these various business cards, letterheads, labels and report covers to the printer for approval—I usually deliver 1200 dpi (dots per inch) plain paper copies for him the following day and he makes his film and plates from it. The quality is usually sufficient for the types of projects he prints.

Then I worked on some design comps for an upcoming annual report. The two-hour project included looking for sample images for backgrounds, which I will later replace with photographs I will shoot specifically for the client.

Next I made some small corrections on an 80-page book/book

cover project, printed out a preview copy for the printer, and PostScripted the file for the service bureau who will be printing it on a docutech because the quantity is too low for regular printing. Then I put it on a zip disk and called a courier.

After that, I went straight to the next job: printing out plain paper composites and separations for the printer's reference on a three-color, four-panel brochure for a local association. I put everything on a disk and called the printer to pick it up.

Lunch was a slice of cold pizza and something sweet. Gotta keep the sugar levels up with the workload I've got! On this day, as usual, I ate while I was working because I never have time to spare.

With the four-panel brochure project wrapped up, I typed and faxed a bid for a two-color 11×17 convention brochure one of my clients requested the previous afternoon. Then I exported some text files from that client's previous product guide which I design for them every year. She will update the listing and E-mail it back so I can insert the copy in this year's guide. I called her to let her know she has text files waiting to be downloaded, and to alert her to look for the bid I have faxed on the brochure.

By 4, I had no less than 14 phone calls from clients who have jobs with deadlines less than two weeks away. Well, actually two of those calls were from fellow desktop publishers asking me if I am as swamped as they are. I made two calls to two different printers to ask for bids on a correspondence card and envelopes for a new client. I also called my annual report client to find out when I'll receive final text so I can begin production. Then I called the book project contact and the four-panel brochure people to let them know that their jobs are wrapped up and on their way to the respective printers.

At this point, I was ready for the next project, about two hours of design and minor changes on an eight-page, two-color tabloid newsletter. The job was done by about 6, and I left it printing, since it's time-consuming for the laser printer, and went to catch the news on TV. When the newsletter was finished printing, I packed it up for a courier to deliver to the client the next morning.

On this particular evening, I went out for dinner. But I was back in the office by 9:30 and worked until midnight paying bills, and typing up invoices for the book project and the brochure that I finished earlier in the day. Then I updated my Quicken account, answered E-mail, and straightened up the office.

Sometimes, though, I get easier days than that when I only put in 12 hours of work.

TONY FRY—Tony Fry & Associates, San Rafael, CA
Before he became independent some thirty years ago, Tony worked as a designer for printing companies, where he got a grounding in printing production. He's been working on the computer since the MacPlus was introduced "with one full megabyte of memory" back in 1986. His specialty is designing direct-mail packages. Tony says that he established regular nine-to-five business hours for himself years ago, and makes it a point not to take on more work than he can handle in that time frame.

I began the day by attending a meeting with a copywriter to discuss some direct-mail projects we will be working on together. When I got back to my own office, I spent most of the rest of the day scanning and retouching (enhancing, tonal correction, outlining and adding drop shadows) some book covers for a catalog of educational materials I am working on. When that was finished, I copied some old projects from my hard drive to zip disks for archival. Then I checked the Internet for prices on a new monitor I intend to acquire. Finally, I prepared an invoice for a completed project and sent it to the client.

ANGELA HAGLUND—Nashville, TN

After a career as a staff designer, Angela decided to go into business for herself in the mid-1990s when she realized she was making more money freelancing. Her business runs the gamut from brochures to catalog inserts to CD covers. Her most unusual job was designing a logo for a dominatrix who answered her ad in a music industry magazine. "I think she had it made into a tattoo," says Angela, "but I don't want to know where it is."

6A.M. Made coffee and started work. I get the most creative work done between 6 and 9, so it's important to choose wisely. On this day, it's a toss-up between the client who has decided to send out a 72-page cookbook in two weeks (and just told me about it yesterday), and another client who just let me know that an ad they are running in *Rolling Stone* is due in less than one week. I opted for the cookbook.

9A.M. Another client called. Could I get him out a Christmas card right away? I had to go to the printer anyway to check press proofs for another client, so I said yes, and made the best Christmas card that I could in an hour.

10A.M. Tried to fax changes in a brochure to a client in Virginia, but the fax machine was acting up. Tried to fax the Christmas card, too, but the machine still wouldn't work.

10:30A.M. Finally got the machine working, got everything faxed and got approval on the Christmas card. Outputted it to a disk, quickly brushed my teeth and picked up the house. We had about half a dozen people coming for a photo shoot in our front yard at 1:30. It looked like rain.

10:45A.M. Arrived at the printer and OK'd the press proofs. Dropped off the Christmas card disk.

11A.M. Our company's Christmas card at another printer has been cut a fraction too large for the envelopes that I oh-so-carefully measured weeks ago. Took back old envelopes. Bought new ones.

11:15A.M. Since I was in the neighborhood, I bought a birthday gift for a friend.

11:30A.M. Back at the house. My planned lunch appointment had to be rushed because the rain was holding off and the photo shoot people seemed to be arriving. Called lunch appointment and ran out to meet them NOW.

12:30–3:15P.M. The rain held off and the photo shoot went off on schedule.

3–4P.M. Various phone calls from different clients as I attempted to typeset the cookbook. The printer called to say that the job was ready. I sent a courier to the printer with a check, then called the client. They were very excited to get the news since this particular printer has dragged this job into a month-long experience from hell.

5:30P.M. The courier arrived back with the job and the client came over. We're a success!

6P.M. Worked out.

7P.M. Took the first shower of the day.

7:30P.M. Went to the computer store to pick up some Zip disks and CD-ROMs.

8:30P.M. Dinner.

SHAWN TEETS—Wordwise, Indianapolis, IN

After working as a technical writer, Shawn discovered desktop publishing in the mid-1990s when she was asked to produce a newsletter on her computer. She creates newsletters, brochures, student papers, and annual reports for individuals, small businesses, and nonprofit organizations, and she works as a consultant on computers and software.

7:30–8A.M. Checked the mailbox on the porch for new projects and, of course, checks.

8–9A.M. Went online to check E-mail, read message boards, and check out some recommended Web sites.

9–9:30A.M. Went to the post office and the bank.

9:30–10A.M. Returned phone calls from the previous day.

10A.M.–NOON Worked on a brochure for a courier service, a résumé for a recent college graduate, and a college student's term paper.

Noon–12:30P.M. Tied up loose ends and checked phone messages.

12:30–1:30P.M. Ate lunch while watching *The Young and the Restless*. (I rarely vary from this step, and if I have deadlines to meet, I record it.)

1:30–2:30P.M. Returned phone calls, checked and answered E-mail messages.

2:30–4P.M. Set up a database for a client's video and compact disk library, and did research on how to standardize input on a client's computer system.

4–5P.M. Took a break and started dinner.

5–6:30P.M. Did software testing for a client on the consulting side of my business. Designed letters from a survey form for my company.

ELLEN CONNOR—Connor Custom Creations, Fayetteville, NC
Ellen got married right out of high school, had two kids and no other career until she learned desktop publishing on her own, and went into the business in the late 1990s. She works with small companies and individuals designing letterheads, business cards, and brochures as well as newsletters and direct-mail pieces. Her education is continuing, and she is becoming an expert in web design. Her days are long, but she is able to spend more time with her children than she would if she worked for someone other than herself. Fortunately, Ellen is "a night person."

I got up at 6 and started my morning in the usual way with coffee and a cinnamon roll. Then I got on the computer, checked my E-mail, and took care of some client correspondence.

At 9, I tuned off the computer and woke the kids for the day. I have a live-in nanny, but the morning is my time with the kids and I like to get them ready for the day and fix their breakfast. After that, they spend the rest of their day with the nanny and I go back to the office.

When I went back to work, I wrote out two invoices for late payments and sent them off to the clients. Then I spent about an hour and a half working on a Web site for a children's' book author.

I took a break for lunch at around noon, and on this particular day the kids and I ordered pizza as a special treat. After lunch I usually spend about two hours signed on to America Online. I get a lot of new clients from messages I post in message boards and newsgroups and business chat rooms.

Around 3, I took another break and spent some more time with the kids—all of this with the phone ringing and answering it with a four-month-old in my arms and a two-year-old screaming for mommy to get off the phone and play.

At about 4, I cleaned up my office, turned on the answering machine and just sat for an hour vegging out.

Nighttime is really when I get the most done. It's funny that I hire a nanny to take care of the kids so I can work at night when they are asleep, but I just can't work a full day without spending half of it with them.

So after I make dinner for my family, and maybe even watch a little television, I am right back on the computer. Last night, I was working from 10 until 4:30 in the morning.

My husband doesn't understand how I live on four hours' sleep each night, and he thinks I'm crazy for doing it. But I love spending time with my kids, and if that means a few extra hours at night, well, it's worth it.

LAURIE PIPER—Presto Press, Austin, Texas

Laurie worked for a managed care organization, publishing fifteen different quarterly state directories. She went into business for herself in 1997, publishing business newsletters. Except when she is on deadline, she generally manages to work a normal eight- or nine-hour day, and even when she is busy, she takes time out of her day for research, which she finds relaxing.

Near the end of every month I work my way through a weeklong deadline for an eight-page parenting newsletter that I publish. My newsletter is distributed through school systems to parents of elementary-age children. During that week, my days are filled with tons of research and writing. Fortunately, I have a template set up in PageMaker that allows me to just flow the text into it.

During this time, I don't do publishing work for anyone else. I have found that my newsletter work soaks up most of my time. But one thing I do almost on a daily basis is explore other people's designs—logos, brochures, book covers. I can't seem to stop analyzing things all around me. I may be at a stop sign and find myself trying to figure out what typeface it is. On a typical day, I will also go online and do some viewing of other design people's Web sites or read through the messages on the message boards.

Except when I'm under deadline, I spend most of my time researching, and just about everything I learn is valuable to my business—finding more of it, getting better at it.

AND THEY WOULDN'T TRADE IT FOR ANYTHING

Every desktop publisher's approach to the average working day varies according to their output and their personality. This is a business that can accommodate a wide variety of lifestyles and work habits, and allows you the choice to work at times when you work best, whether it is first thing in the morning or the middle of the night. Even though many seem to work punishing hours, it is usually because they choose to. They work for themselves and they like what they do. And although their workdays vary, they all agree: They wouldn't trade their life for anything else. Cindy Dyer says, "I never thought I'd ever be self-employed, but now that I'm off on my own, I'd never go back." Susan Abbott appreciates the opportunity to "do stuff with my daughter." And she believes that her decision to become a desktop publisher "is the best thing I've ever done in my life." Ellen Connor says that her only regret is "that I waited so long to get started."

CHAPTER FOUR

Thinking It Through

Many desktop publishers use their past work experience to create their new business. Whether that experience was in the graphic arts or in fast and accurate word handling, most agree that desktop publishing opens the door to both creative and financial independence. But before you hang out your own shingle, take an honest look at what experience you'll be bringing to the table.

Chris Petrone, a desktop publisher in Bedford, New York, used his experience to build a solid business in the sales promotion field. He produces brochures, package inserts, point-of-sale materials, and other printed pieces whose aim is to make an actual sale. Chris worked for sixteen years as both an art director and creative director at New York City advertising agencies. In the 1970s, when most ad agencies were steering their clients into television advertising, Chris gravitated toward sales promotion agencies because he found more satisfaction working with print. Advertising philosophy eventually began to change, and he found himself in the right place at the right time because he had experience on both sides of the street—sales promotion and advertising.

"Most designers didn't know anything about marketing, and they knew even less about the synergy between advertising and promotion," he says. "And whenever I went out to call on one of the agency's clients, they were astounded that I did." The comment he heard most often in those days was "Where did you come from?," but the message he was getting pointed him in a new direction. The time was ripe to use his experience to the best advantage and go into business for himself.

Richie Minor, who owns a service bureau in Evansville, Indiana, once sold computers for a living. His enthusiasm for the things he was selling turned him into an unabashed computer freak or, as he describes it, "a nerd with an attitude." It led him away from the sales floor to a job with a service bureau, where he found more challenges, and eventually an opportunity to open his own shop. Along the way he developed a reputation as a skilled troubleshooter. "Printers, desktop publishers, even my competitors, send their nightmare jobs and hell files to me," he boasts, "and I love 'em."

EXPLORE THE MARKET

Before Richie Minor started his business, there were two service bureaus in Evansville, the one he worked for and the local newspaper that took on outside work but usually ignored the deadlines of all clients except its own advertisers. When Richie's boss sold the business to an advertising agency and the agency's regular clients began getting first crack at its services, it was apparent that the town needed an independent service bureau. And it was apparent to Richie that he had the know-how to put one together. He had become a walking encyclopedia on the equipment involved and what it could accomplish; he knew who his clients would be and he knew the kind of service for which they were desperate. Most important, he knew that the competition was handing him a golden opportunity.

Richie's gut feeling told him that he could make it on his own, but he didn't just jump in with both feet. Even though it seemed obvious there was a need for someone like him, he put together a detailed business plan that included a thorough study of the market. This is the first step that anyone starting a new business should take.

PLAN FOR SUCCESS

After Richie was convinced that his business plan could work, he used it to convince a financial backer that he had a future. And by following his plan closely, he managed to pay the money back in less than a year.

After three years in business, Richie began putting together a new plan—he decided to use his knack for teaching to start up a computer training school, with local schools and colleges as eager prospects.

You may have a gut feeling that you can make a success of desktop publishing. And since you probably aren't planning to open a service bureau and don't need the big start-up investment Richie was faced with, it may seem easier to just go ahead and wing it. *Don't even think of it.*

Before you make any plans, analyze your strengths and your weaknesses, your past experience and your talents. Take a personal inventory of what works for you and what doesn't, and think about what you expect from the future.

The reality is that as a desktop publisher you'll be selling yourself more than anything else, which is why *you* are the most important thing to consider.

ASK THE EXPERTS

Don't you wish you knew a retired executive who's been there before and wants to share the experiences of a lifetime? Well, there is one just around the corner waiting for your call.

An agency of the Small Business Administration called the Service Corps of Retired Executives (SCORE for short) specializes in helping people like you. These volunteers can tell you just about everything you need to know about starting up a new business and keeping it alive. One of them will know exactly how to put together a business plan, and the consultation won't cost you a dime.

You'll find the nearest SCORE office listed under "U.S. Government" in the telephone book along with the numbers for the Small Business Administration. You'll also find the agency on the Internet under the keyword SBA. All of its services are free, and they're all designed to help you make your business work.

SCORE has more than three hundred offices across the country, manned by more than thirteen thousand volunteers, all of whom are seasoned business veterans. It isn't very likely you're going to find a retired desktop publisher in any of them, of course—this business is too new for that—but there are basic rules that apply to every small business and SCORE's volunteers are on hand every business day to show you how those rules can affect yours.

Most desktop publishers are creative people who often find dealing with financial details difficult if not boring, but it goes without saying that when you're in business for yourself, keeping your eye on your finances is a matter of life and death. The people at SCORE will help you with the financial aspects of your business, not just at the beginning, but down the road as well.

YOUR INITIAL INVESTMENT

In terms of your initial start-up investment, some of the rules that apply to other small businesses may not apply in your case. In a world where the price of everything is always going up, prices for computers, peripherals, and programs are actually going down, for instance.

A few years ago, a desktop publisher in the Southeast started his business with a high-end workstation that cost him twelve thousand dollars. Three years later, the price for completely replacing it had dropped to four thousand dollars. But there is another number to consider. The resale value of his original workstation had plummeted to eight hundred dollars in those same three years. And because of numbers like that, lending institutions rarely make loans to buy the computer equipment that is the heart and soul of a desktop publishing business.

On the other hand, getting started as a desktop publisher isn't nearly as expensive as opening a drugstore or setting up a bed-and-breakfast. You may already have a decent computer and accumulated most of the peripherals and software it will take to handle your clients' needs at the beginning. And you may be planning to start out with a home office, which will also help to keep your start-up costs down.

Kevin Edwards, a Duluth, Georgia, desktop publisher, says that he visited his local SCORE office before he left his day job, and when the conversation turned to money, he says, ". . . they told me that I'd have to settle for an 'F&F' loan. When I asked what that meant, the man smiled and said, 'friends and family.' " Kevin took the advice and turned to his parents. Others who didn't share a resource like that have used their credit cards to start out with the bare essentials, and as business came their way, they added more. Although experiences vary, desktop publishers seem, on average, to become cash positive in six months to a year, and most plow their profits back into the business.

But not all desktop publishers have to wait that long. Mark Robinson's Markworks Graphic Design in Torrance, California, was making money for him from the first day. He started the business more than a dozen years ago with his own savings, and he says that most other people he knows started out the same way, even if not all of them were able to start paying themselves back quite so quickly.

MAKING IT WORK FOR YOU

Alon Feder, who started Key Advertising Concepts in San Diego in the late 1980s, believes that beginning with a personal inventory is one of the keys to success. "It takes confidence and courage to make it in this business," he says. "You can learn about good design if you study, and with experience comes better design and, hopefully, a better ability to move around in the business world.

"But take my word for it, it's not an easy process to venture out on your own. Some people might have a completely natural ability to start their own desktop publishing business and make a big bang right away—although I find this is rarely the case. Personally, I have always been highly independent. But it can get pretty scary when you don't pick up a paycheck every week or so. The income flows with the tides, and if you can't channel those tides, you have to be able to ride them out.

". . . Anyone can start doing computer graphic design by buying a computer and some software," he adds, "but what is that person doing to bring himself into the picture and make a difference?"

IS THIS BUSINESS RIGHT FOR YOU?

Bringing yourself into the picture has less to do with your personality than with your attitude. You may think of yourself as an entrepreneurial type, and that can surely be an asset when you go into business for yourself, but things like self-discipline and organization, attention to detail, dealing with people, and occasionally doing things you may not enjoy are what will determine your success.

Try the following questionnaire written by Charles L. Sodikoff, Ph.D., a psychologist and career management professional who has counseled people like you for the last fifteen years. It will add

to your understanding of whether you have the ability and willingness to go off on your own.

PROFILE FOR SUCCESS

Take a minute to circle the numbers that apply to you:

Ability to Do
4 = Real strength
3 = Able to do
2 = Need to work on
1 = Real weakness

Willingness to Do
4 = Really like doing
3 = Not a problem
2 = Do not want to do
1 = Will not do

	Ability to Do	Willingness to Do
Managing your own time	4 3 2 1	4 3 2 1
Organizing your day	4 3 2 1	4 3 2 1
Working long hours	4 3 2 1	4 3 2 1
Working on weekends	4 3 2 1	4 3 2 1
Putting personal and family plans on hold	4 3 2 1	4 3 2 1
Meeting people/ talking to strangers	4 3 2 1	4 3 2 1
Mixing business and social activities	4 3 2 1	4 3 2 1
Selling yourself to others	4 3 2 1	4 3 2 1
Selling products or services	4 3 2 1	4 3 2 1
Working with demanding or difficult customers/ clients	4 3 2 1	4 3 2 1
Managing the work of others	4 3 2 1	4 3 2 1
Dealing with employee problems	4 3 2 1	4 3 2 1

	Ability to Do	Willingness to Do
Terminating employees when necessary	4 3 2 1	4 3 2 1
Initiating new projects	4 3 2 1	4 3 2 1
Working on own without having others to share ideas	4 3 2 1	4 3 2 1
Setting long-range goals and specific targets	4 3 2 1	4 3 2 1
Taking a planned and organized approach to work	4 3 2 1	4 3 2 1
Juggling multiple tasks at one time	4 3 2 1	4 3 2 1
Doing clerical tasks	4 3 2 1	4 3 2 1
Working under tight deadlines	4 3 2 1	4 3 2 1
Looking for creative solutions to problems	4 3 2 1	4 3 2 1
Making difficult decisions	4 3 2 1	4 3 2 1
Solving problems on the spot	4 3 2 1	4 3 2 1
Dealing with uncertainty	4 3 2 1	4 3 2 1
Having patience to "stick-with-it" through slow periods	4 3 2 1	4 3 2 1
Investing your own money	4 3 2 1	4 3 2 1
Taking financial risks	4 3 2 1	4 3 2 1
Understanding and maintaining financial records	4 3 2 1	4 3 2 1

SCORING
ABILITY TO DO

If you gave yourself scores of 1 or 2 on three or more items, you need to carefully examine how those things are going to get done when you are in business for yourself.

First determine, in the areas where you scored low, how important they are to the type of desktop publishing business you are planning. A word processing operation may not require the same range of abilities as a graphics-oriented one. But if they appear to be essential, are you going to be able to learn them?

WILLINGNESS TO DO

If you gave yourself scores of 1 or 2 on three or more items in this column, you need to carefully examine your level of commitment to your new business.

Examine each problem area, keeping in mind how likely you will encounter these issues in your specific business. If these are things you know must get done, and you aren't going to be happy doing them, then you must ask yourself one more question: Why do you want to go into the desktop publishing business?

BE HONEST WITH YOURSELF

You may be able to fool all of the people some of the time and some of the people all of the time, but the one person you can never fool is yourself. Of course, you are eager to have your own business, but when you are making plans to go out on your own, be sure you do it with your eyes wide open. You're planning your own future, and this is no time for anything less than honest soul searching.

CHAPTER FIVE

Defining Your Business

The kind of work you'll turn out with your desktop publishing business will have a lot to do with your location. Before you decide whether to go into business or not, take a close look at what's around you. There may be unnoticed opportunities out there or competition you weren't expecting. Gather as much information as you can about the market, the competition, and how you're going to fit into the mix. You can never do too much research when you're planning your new venture—you don't want to find yourself explaining in hindsight why it didn't work. Gather the information *before* you start.

Alon Feder, who is thriving as a designer in the large and relatively crowded market of San Diego, says that the first questions anyone starting out needs to ask are: "How many people out there are doing what you want to do? Is the market glutted? Are there a lot of people with a lot of experience, or are there a lot of entry-level design candidates who will work for less just to get the experience? How much do you want to be paid, and how much are others being paid for the same kind of work?"

Before Cindy Dyer became a desktop publisher, most of her working years were spent in Washington, D.C., where she began to notice that there were opportunities for a computer-literate designer such as herself. But it was also apparent to her that it wouldn't be long before D.C. would be filled with such people, so she moved down the Potomac to the fertile ground of Alexandria, Virginia. For her, the strategy worked.

But, then, sometimes, staying put can make all the difference. Shawn Teets, whose Indianapolis, Indiana, company, Wordwise, specializes in newsletters, brochures, and business reports, has done a lot of business with national sororities and fraternities that are based in her hometown. It was an opportunity she might have missed when the company she worked for as a technical writer relocated to Florida. When she decided not to go with them, the firm kept her on as a telecommuter. They installed a computer, fax machine, and black-and-white laser printer in her home and she went right on working for them.

When an organization she belonged to asked her to produce its newsletter, she found the work fascinating and decided to look for more jobs like it. But there was a problem. The equipment she was using wasn't hers. She solved it by bartering unused vacation and sick time for it, quit her job as a technical writer, and became independent. One of her first clients was her former Florida-based boss, who was struggling to produce a family newsletter to keep in touch with the folks back home in Indiana.

Thanks to fax machines, overnight courier services and the Internet, many desktop publishers routinely work, with clients hundreds or even thousands of miles away. When Angela Haglund found that her freelance design work was producing more income than her regular job, she decided to quit the job and go out on her own. She started off in style, producing a four-color insert for a catalog producer in Arizona. Although Angela lives in Nashville, the distance between her and her client didn't make any difference at all. Today, she is branching out into cyberspace by designing Web sites, but the bulk of her business, after more than two years as an independent desktop publisher, is designing CD covers for the music industry right around the corner. "I do tons of them," she says, "but it wasn't what I was planning when I started out. It just happened."

WHO'S YOUR COMPETITION?

Before she started out, Angela assumed that the music publishers in Nashville already had established sources for their design needs. It turned out she was wrong, and her business went off in an unanticipated direction. It was a happy accident, to be sure, but suppose she had gone into business assuming that the musicians would beat a path to her door and then discovered their doors were closed? Don't assume anything. Before you start, make it a point to find out who your customers are likely to be, and, just as important, who is serving them now and at what price.

When Kevin Edwards went into the desktop publishing business in Duluth, Georgia, he began by making a lot of cold calls looking for what he calls "down and dirty work," small jobs like business cards that can lead to bigger orders. But he says he often ran into stone walls when prospects told him, "We've got a lady who does this kind of stuff for us from her home. And she does it dirt cheap." It was a very important discovery that helped him alter his strategies and leave the down and dirty stuff to others. He soon found that there was plenty of better work to be done, and by raising his sights he became the one who was doing it.

It's essential to know who your competitors are before you go into business for yourself. It can help you determine what's missing in your neighborhood and whether there is a service in short supply that you can translate into your own niche business.

FINDING A NICHE

It is imperative that you establish a niche before you go into business. Without it you have no realistic way of finding the work you need in order to get a solid start. Of course, your business will evolve over time, but you won't get off the ground unless you first figure out exactly what your core business will be.

For a few years, Cindy Dyer worked as an art director for a consulting firm, retail companies, and trade associations. She was amazed at how few freelance designers seemed interested in learning the computer, something she herself had done on the job. There was an opportunity there, and she took advantage of it to open her own desktop publishing business in 1985. "I was filling a void," she claims. But before she went off on her own, Cindy took a job with a temporary agency to add to her computer skills and to make contacts in Alexandria, Virginia, where she had relocated. The contacts were valuable, and she's still doing work for some of them today, but her first job was for her supervisor at the temp agency. He was planning to become independent, too, but as a travel agent, and he hired her to design a brochure, letterheads, and business cards for him.

LET YOUR NICHE EVOLVE

Although doing "tons of CD covers" is Angela Haglund's stock-in-trade right now, and she's pleased with the volume, she has an eye on a completely different niche. She's betting that her new interest in designing Web sites will be her primary business before long. She believes that the basic knowledge that most of her potential competitors have is limited to HTML—HyperText Markup Language, the technical side of creating web pages. "Not very many of them seem to know anything about design, and there is a big need out there for people who do." Her original niche is still supporting her, but her business is growing in a new direction.

When Shawn Teets started out, she attracted business by doing better-quality work than her competitors. But then she discovered that she could expand her niche by doing it faster. Every desktop publisher has clients who want their jobs delivered "yesterday." It's an old tradition that was in place long before computers came on the scene. In Shawn's case, the desperate ones are usually students who forget about papers they need until the deadline is right on top of them. She has a special rush rate for procrastinators, but, she says, "when I quote it, customers usually decide they weren't in such a terrible hurry after all." She's saved the day for enough people that word of her reputation for speedy service has gotten around.

Shawn also discovered that she has a knack for the world of high-tech, and has built an unexpected niche for herself computer consulting and testing software.

Cindy Dyer created a niche by using her own photographs to add value to the jobs she produces. Most desktop publishers use stock photography to illustrate their pieces, but because Cindy is a professional photographer as well as a designer, she is able to personalize her work with original images. It not only sets her apart from the competition, but, as she describes it, "going out on a shoot breaks my normal routine, and because they usually want to go along, it gives me a chance to spend some time getting to know my clients better."

The endless variety of things the computer allows you to do is the biggest advantage of a desktop publishing business. From designing Web sites to producing business forms, four-color brochures, Santa letters, résumés, newsletters, and everything in between, there is no limit to the things you can accomplish. The trick, of course, is to do it better than your competitors. That is the best kind of niche you can find.

PUT A BUSINESS PLAN TOGETHER

After you've gathered all the information you can about your potential clients, your competition, and how your business fits, the next step is to get it all down on paper. Your business plan may be the most important document you'll ever produce as a desktop publisher.

The people at SCORE can help you get started, and will help you refine your business plan as you go along. Every business plan begins with a few basic questions about your potential customers, your ability to serve them, and what the competition is. Your plan will need to include a realistic way to make your business grow once you've become established. And it needs to address the options open to you if your plan doesn't work.

But to make it work, you're going to need to assess your financial picture *before* you make a decision to go off on your own and it should be included in your plan. You may not have an immediate answer to all of the questions in the following questionnaire, written by career guidance professional Charles L. Sodikoff, Ph.D. If you don't, ask your accountant or your friend at SCORE for help. Your financial analysis will be at the heart of your business plan.

DON'T LEAVE ANY STONES UNTURNED

Be specific and detailed with your answers; they should make sense to a stranger. A plan based on dreams and not reality isn't worth the time it takes to write it. Make sure your plan isn't so rigid that it can't be changed after you've started your business or that it isn't too vague to be helpful. Your business plan should tell you, and anyone else who reads it, exactly where you are going—and, much more important, how you expect to get there.

The easiest way to begin writing your business plan is to take a short vacation. Alone. Take along a bunch of yellow legal pads, a few pens, and an open mind. Then, as you relax by a pool, on a beach, or next to a river or stream, take a hard look at where you want the future to take you. Go ahead and dream, but be completely honest with yourself. What you put on paper is going to help you follow your dream, and the last thing you

FINANCIAL READINESS

- What is the proper structure your business should have? Should it be a sole proprietorship, a partnership, a limited liability company, or a corporation?
- How much money will it take to get your business started? What will you need to invest in equipment and supplies, setting up an office, advertising and promotion, fees and software?
- Where are you going to get the money? Have you explored all the alternatives with a financial expert?
- How much income do you need to support yourself (and your family) every month?
- How long do you anticipate it is going to take for your business to begin making a profit?
- How will you support yourself (and your family) until the business becomes profitable? How long can you support yourself this way?
- How much overhead can your business afford?
- Will you need to hire others now or in the future? What level of expertise is needed? How much payroll will you be able to afford? Will you need to provide insurance?
- How well do you understand: Bookkeeping principles? Cash flow? Balance sheets? Profit-and-loss-statements? Sales forecasting?
- How well do you know your market? Who is going to buy your services?
- Who is your competition? What will you do if more competitors arrive on the scene?
- How will you charge for your services? What are your competitors charging?
- How will you deal with clients who don't pay you on time? Or not at all?

need is to have your path skewed by things you didn't really believe.

START WITH THE OBVIOUS

Some of the questions you'll be asking yourself may seem pretty obvious, like: What sort of business am I planning? and What services am I going to offer? But ask them anyway; no detail is too insignificant.

Other considerations you should get into writing are why there is a need for this business of yours, where you are going to find your customers, and how much can you expect them to pay for your services.

You'll also need to make notes on the computer equipment and software you have, what you're going to need, and what it all will probably cost. And don't forget to include the investment you already have in the things you bought before you began dreaming this dream of yours.

If you're planning to work from home—and some 60 percent of all desktop publishers do—think about what it's going to cost you to create and furnish your home office. Even if you've already converted the front porch, write it down.

You should also record what you've found out about the other desktop publishers lurking around your neighborhood. And what you're going to offer that's better. Then you need to think about what kind of advertising and marketing you're going to use to lure their customers away and find others of your own.

THINK ABOUT THE MONEY

The most important thing you should consider is your financial plan, not just for this year but for at least five years into the future. Begin by estimating your start-up costs—such things as telephone deposits, software and hardware, fees and licenses.

Then project your operating costs. Include supplies, utility bills, taxes, legal fees, accounting services, insurance, and the freelance help you may find you need. You'll need to plan for printing bills and service bureau fees and for the costs of upgrading your computer system and software in this ever-changing world of technology.

And whatever you do, don't forget your living expenses.

Now, think about the money you can expect to make. Break down the business you anticipate on a weekly and monthly basis and translate those estimates into income statements. From there you can determine your break-even point, predict profits, and avoid cash flow problems.

Keep in mind that cash flow is what you're going to need to stay alive and ahead of the bill collectors. Profits help your business grow—be sure you have planned for them.

CHAPTER SIX

Getting Started

It's obvious that you are going to need a computer, and you may already have a suitable one. But if you're shopping for a new system, the right choices may not be so obvious.

Although you probably have a good idea of the kind of work you expect your equipment to do, make it a point to talk with some prospective clients to find out what *they* expect. And before you invest in anything, know what kind of material your service bureau and printer are set up to interface with and what they're going to expect you to provide. Remember, the service bureau is going to translate the files you produce into material the printer will need to actually produce the job. If your computer or your software isn't compatible with theirs, you're going to have a big problem.

It's a good bet, though, that none of you will be able to predict what those expectations are likely to be a year or two from now. The markets for independent desktop publishers may be growing fast, but the computer field itself is growing even faster. When you become a desktop publisher, most of your clients will be people who have their own businesses to watch, and they'll expect you to keep an eye on the technology.

Be cautious when you begin investing in the tools of the trade. New or revised hardware and software is being developed every day, so it's wise to concentrate on the things you need to get started. But at all times, keep the following two things in mind: compatibility and upgrade capability.

A SHOPPING LIST

If you were born to shop, you've picked the right field. Prices vary from catalog to catalog and from store to store—where you may even find that the price on the shelf is negotiable! It's a good idea to shop around, but bargains aren't the only thing you should be looking for. A computer that's short on memory or isn't compatible with the software you need now or in the future isn't worth the space it takes up on your desk.

When you set off on your shopping excursion, you're going to meet some computer salespeople who will remind you of used car salesmen, which may be why the industry calls them "resellers." Sure, you can expect them to know a lot about their products and you can learn a lot by listening to them, but don't let them talk you into buying things you don't need or can't use. Do your homework first. Talk with people who use computers as well as people who sell them. Take a trip on the Internet and visit computer-related websites. Read computer magazines and newspapers and send away for information from their advertisers—and, by the way, a fellow desktop publisher probably designed the things you'll get back in the mail.

WHAT SHOULD IT BE: MAC OR PC?

Using a service such as America Online or MSN will lead you to chats, forums, and message boards loaded with information and opinions on the things you need before you start your business. But one question that will never get you a simple answer is whether to buy a Macintosh or a PC system. This is something you need to know before you begin. But watch out, the people who prefer one over the other are like religious fanatics, and they'll do everything possible to convert you to their way of thinking.

In general, PC people will tell you that they prefer IBM and its clones because there are more programs available for them. That may be true, but desktop publishers who deal with design usually prefer Macintosh, which handles the programs they need more easily. But, then again, since the development of Microsoft Windows, the graphics capabilities of PCs have become more like Macs.

Still, emotion runs high in the two camps. Karen Cunningham, whose work mostly involves word processing, swears by her IBM-compatible machine, as do many desktop publishers who don't do a lot of graphics work. And thanks to Windows, she says she, too, is able to handle graphics and layouts without going to the trouble of learning the Macintosh platform. On the other hand, graphics designer Kevin Edwards says that people who prefer PCs are "just kidding themselves. . . . The most experienced designers can make them work, but the rest just can't." As the saying goes, "You pays your money and you takes your choice."

When all is said and done, the choice you make is a highly personal one, and may depend on the kind of hardware you may own and have already mastered. But it is *imperative* to check that the system you choose is compatible with the systems your clients own, your service bureau uses, and your printer prefers. Converting files can take time, and that cost will be passed along to you.

BUY OR LEASE?

But, then again, you may not have to *buy* either platform. You can lease your equipment on a weekly, monthly, or yearly basis through a computer rental firm, which you'll find in the Yellow

Pages or through direct-sales companies like Dell and Gateway, who are also beginning to offer leasing options. Leasing could be a good way to road-test a machine you're thinking of buying. And, if something breaks down, as it inevitably will, you may be glad to turn your problem over to the leasing company.

In general, leasing costs more than buying, but it's a way to spread your investment costs into convenient monthly payments. When tax time rolls around, your lease payments are a business expense you can deduct, but, conversely, when you own your own equipment, you can take a tax deduction for depreciation. But depending on where you live (tax laws vary from state to state), you may find that the bigger tax break will come on your leased equipment. Check with your accountant—you might be in for a pleasant surprise.

Another factor to consider is that computer equipment has the life expectancy of a butterfly. If your system is two years old, there is probably one on the market with twice the megs, but if you're strapped for cash you'll have to resign yourself to getting along with what you've got. It's why big companies make it a point to lease technology rather than buy it. It keeps their credit in line and saves their working capital. When you start up your own business your needs are different than that of the average consumer. For the consumer, the higher costs of leasing probably isn't the way to go, but for you it might make sense to preserve your cash flow.

Many computer leasing companies also offer an option to buy the hardware you rent, but this is probably more expensive than buying it in the first place. On the other hand, some lease agreements will allow you to swap your obsolete equipment for upgraded models at the end of the contract. Either way, be sure the dealer offers convenient, speedy, and reliable service. When your computer isn't working, you're out of business.

A good argument for leasing is Moore's Law, formulated back in 1965 by Intel's Gordon Moore, who said that the performance of computer chips doubles every eighteen months. It was proven true for more than thirty years, but new breakthroughs in chip technology have begun changing all the rules, including that one. As they continue improving at an unprecedented rate, the hardware you buy today could be obsolete before you take it out of the box.

If owning your own hardware makes better sense to you, computer magazines usually do a good job of keeping ahead of new developments and preview the capabilities of newer hardware before it reaches the stores. A little research before you go shopping might help you get more for your money and will most certainly help you choose the system that is right for you.

LEARN THE JARGON

As in most other fields, the computer business has a language all its own and, like traveling in a foreign country, it's a good idea to learn a few of the key words before beginning your tour of the land of the resellers.

THE BASIC COMPUTER

The most basic of the terms in computerspeak is CPU. It is the central processing unit that makes software able to do its job. Its main storage area is a fixed internal magnetic disk known as a hard drive, which most desktop publishers agree can never have too much memory. These days, hard drive memory is usually measured in gigabytes (GB on the spec sheets), which translates as a billion bytes. In a 1997 survey of its subscribers, *Publish* magazine found that the average respondent's system contained 2.6 gigabytes of hard drive space, and that more than half of them said they planned to add more in the next year, bringing their storage capacity up to 4.8 gigs. Some of today's computers come loaded with memory. For example, although most new

Macs range from 1 GB to 4 GB, one of the PowerMac models starts out with 9 gigabytes in its hard drive.

ABOUT BITS AND BYTES

And what, you might ask, is a byte? It's a combination of adjacent bits that form a character—which means one letter, number, or punctuation mark. A bit, also called a binary digit, is the single basic unit of information fed into a computer.

Floppy disks and other storage devices with a capacity of less than a million characters are measured in kilobytes, a thousand at a time, designated by an upper-case K (800K = 800,000 bytes). Above a million bytes, the designation becomes M or MB for megabytes.

DON'T FORGET TO CHECK THE RAM

One of the ways megabytes will haunt you as a desktop publisher is when it relates to RAM, random access memory. Design programs eat up those MGs (megs) like salted nuts. When you shop for a computer, look for the highest amount of RAM you can afford and then look beyond that number to see how much more memory can be added later. You're going to need it. A survey in *Publish* magazine reveals that 58.1 MGs of RAM was average when the questionnaires were filled out at the end of 1997. It's anybody's guess what's average today.

It isn't always necessary to start with your computer loaded to the gills. A couple of years ago, Kevin Edwards spent almost nine hundred dollars to upgrade his RAM by 82 megabytes. Exactly a year later, the price for the same upgrade had dropped to three hundred dollars, and it would cost even less today. Prices are constantly falling for just about everything a desktop publisher needs, and this is especially true of memory. If you can't spring for a lot of extra money up-front, make sure that you'll be able to add it later when you can afford it.

STORAGE DEVICES

Nothing in the day-to-day operation of a desktop publishing is as important as backing up files, so while you're shopping, add a "superfloppy" storage system, such as a zip, to your list. A zip drive makes it easy to store and back up files, and is often the best way to send your work to the service bureau and printer. A drive costs under one hundred fifty dollars and the disks are about fifteen dollars apiece.

You might also make a removable cartridge drive, such as a jaz, a top priority after you get started. The drive will cost between four and six hundred dollars, but it allows you to store a gigabyte of information on each disk, and to transport the biggest of files. Better still, it's a handy way to back up your entire hard drive. Naturally, jaz cartridges are pricey (from seventy-five to one hundred dollars), but the convenience and peace of mind are worth it.

As a desktop publisher, you probably don't have to be told how important it is to be fanatical about backing up your work, but sometimes an electrical storm, a power surge, or even a power failure can catch you by surprise. For that reason, you absolutely must have your computer plugged into a surge protector. Even better, consider buying an uninterrupted power supply (UPS). For as little as a hundred dollars, it will protect your whole system from those random catastrophies—your CPU, your printer, your modem, your fax machine, and your storage drives. In addition, it suppresses surges in your telephone line when you're online. Many models will also automatically save data and shut down the computer when the power fails.

THE MONITOR

Your window on the world of desktop publishing is the monitor. It also, say some design professionals, needs to be big—21 inches big. But the price is big, too, and if you're on a tight budget, it might be prudent for you to consider going down to 17 inches. Before you do, though, there is another word you need to know about, pixels (picture elements), the smallest part of an image that can be processed. Newer monitors are capable of displaying large numbers of pixels, but in spite of that, screens smaller than 17 inches don't have the capability of showing tiny details and may not be practical for some of the work you intend to do.

Although a 21-inch or larger screen is the Holy Grail of desktop publishers who do design work, those who do word processing find they don't need a picture that big. Still, even they prefer working with larger screens that allow them to view bigger segments of a document at one time. But no matter what their specialty, many do very nicely with smaller ones. Kevin Edwards, for instance, never switched from the 15-inch monitor that came with his Macintosh Performa. Tony Fry is planning to upgrade his 17-inch screen, but only to 19 inches, not 21. "I can't afford anything bigger," he says. But he thinks the larger screen will be better for him because "scrolling time adds up on you." He also finds that the pallets that appear on the screen with graphics software cut down on the amount of working space he has.

In general, if you buy a 17-inch monitor rather than the larger 21 inches, you'll get about half the pixels. But it will cost about half as much. And there are some other advantages to consider. The tube in your monitor, often called a CRT (cathode ray tube), is a cousin of the one in your TV set, and the bigger it gets, the less sharp it is and the harder it is to control color and focus.

All CRTs have a thin metal mask that trains a beam of electrons to phosphors on the front of the screen, but you'll have a choice of different kinds. While shadow-mask monitors have phosphor dots, aperture-grille monitors, such as Sony's Trinitron, contain phosphor stripes. There are other variations on the theme, and they all look different, but in the end what you should concentrate on is a bright, sharp image across the whole screen area. Remember that anything less can cause eyestrain.

You're going to hear a lot of terminology when you go monitor shopping and the spec sheets will have some information the salesperson might forget to mention. Among them are dot, grille, and mask pitch, all of which refer to the distance between the dots or stripes on the screen. The smaller the number, the better the resolution and the sharper the image.

Another term you'll hear is refresh rate, but take that one with a grain of salt. It refers to the monitor's capability to display an image repeatedly so it won't fade; but that is usually a function of the computer's circuitry, and not the monitor. You should, though, look for a high refresh rate on bigger screens. The number will refer to the number of times per second the electron gun at the back of the monitor can scan the screen. It is usually expressed as Hertz, and in this case, the higher the number the better.

KEYBOARDS

The keyboard you select—and there are dozens of different kinds to choose from—is strictly a matter of what's most comfortable for your hands. Obviously, the best way to determine that is to try them out before you decide to buy. And because you're going to be using it constantly, it's well worth investing in a hand-rest or a keyboard that has one built into it. It's the best way to avoid carpal tunnel syndrome, a painful disorder of wrist nerves—one of the occupational hazards of using a computer.

THE MOUSE

It's hard to improve on something as simple as a mouse, but that doesn't stop computer makers from trying. Some professionals prefer trackballs because they take up less desk space, and they say they're faster. Others like joystick devices, possibly because it makes them feel like race-car drivers or astronauts. It's your call. In the end, the mouse you buy depends on its comfort factor. It also is a very personal choice, but, remember, that mouse is going to be your constant companion.

PRINTERS AND OTHER PERIPHERALS

If you went out to buy a car in the early 1950s, the heater was an optional extra and you would have had to pay extra to have one installed. In the computer business these days, optional extras are called peripherals, and some of them, like those car heaters, are things you really can't do without.

The term doesn't seem to apply to something as basic to desktop publishing as a printer, for instance. Printers can reproduce in black-and-white or color, and they come in three types—dot-matrix, inkjet, and laser. The print quality of dot-matrix printers tends to be ragged and they are not recommended for desktop publishing. Besides, as the cost of better-quality inkjet printers keeps dropping, dot-matrix printers are quickly on their way to the museum. You still see them in computer stores and catalogs because they are excellent for printing multiple-copy forms as well as checks, receipts, and other business documents. A dot-matrix printer is a lot like an old-fashioned typewriter, right down to the ribbon.

Though most consider the laser printer best, many desktop publishers get good results with their inkjets, either black-and-white or color, for outputting proofs. A good-quality color inkjet printer is priced in the two-hundred-dollar range, and prices for color laser printers are well over three times as expensive and get more so as quality increases.

There are many variations on the inkjet theme as newer technology brings them closer to laser quality. Among the leaders in this quest for more color and realism is the Canon Corporation, whose bubble jet printers print color photographs almost as close to the original as the output of more expensive laser printers.

If you get an inkjet printer, make sure you have a spare ink cartridge in your desk. These printers spray ink onto the page from a sealed cartridge, but very few will warn you when they're running dry. They just spew out blank pages as if nothing has happened.

Like a Xerox machine, a laser printer uses a laser diode to transfer an image to a cylindrical drum that in turn uses an electrostatic process to attract toner particles (the powder that creates the printout) that are fused to the page by heated rollers. The best, and most expensive, of them is PostScript, which has its own CPU and memory as well as its own built-in type fonts.

The key to quality in selecting a laser printer is dpi, dots per inch. The most common is 300 dpi, which is adequate for producing letters and many basic desktop publishing jobs. But if you're going to print small or decorative type, or photos where shades of gray are important, you ought to consider 600 dpi, which will give you reproduction that's not twice as sharp, as you might expect, but four times as sharp. It's more expensive, of course, but like everything else in the computer field, prices keep dropping.

Cindy Dyer, who produces magazines and books, annual reports and newsletters, uses an $8^{1}/_{2} \times 11$ black-and-white laser PostScript printer for proofing and for final output on smaller jobs. She also has an inkjet color printer that she uses for creating color proofs. In her opinion, after more than a dozen years in the business, "most designers/desktop publishers will never need anything higher than that."

CD-ROMS

For desktop publishing, your computer should also have a CD-ROM drive. That's shorthand for "compact disk read-only memory." A lot of the software you'll need is delivered only on compact disks, not to mention type fonts, clip art, and photographic images. Not too long ago, CD-ROM capability was one of those "optional" peripherals, but computers generally come equipped with them these days. In any case, they are not optional in desktop publishing.

SCANNERS

A flatbed scanner is also considered basic equipment for a desktop publisher. It's the tool that allows you to import images into your computer so they can be integrated into the jobs you are producing. Some scanners read only black-and-white and grayscale images, and cost less than those that scan color. But color scanners are much more practical for desktop publishers, and they don't cost much more. There are many choices, and yours will depend on the kind of work you'll make your specialty. But don't buy any kind of scanner until you've had a chance to look at its actual output and not what the brochure says it can do.

A new breed of flatbed scanner not only gets the images into your computer, but doubles as a laser printer, copier, and a fax machine, too. When you're shopping for one, remember that a copier and a printer aren't the same thing. All scanners function as copiers, but only the more expensive ones also incorporate a printer. You can also use them to scan text into your computer. A budget version of this multitalented machine is priced well below three hundred dollars, but even the best of them come in at around a thousand.

If you are planning to work with images on film or with slides, adapters are available that allow some flatbed scanners to read them, but for better quality you might consider a slide scanner. A flatbed scanner converts images into pixels by reflecting light off the original, but a slide scanner passes light through the film, which results in sharper detail. Apart from the fact that they are expensive, slide scanners are limited to film, and you can't use them to scan anything on a piece of paper unless you make a slide of it first.

In general, a scanner translates images into pixels, and if you are going to be dealing with a lot of text, you ought to add an OCR (optical character recognition) program that will allow your computer to tell the difference between words and pictures. When it does, it will create a text file that you can import into your word processing program. When you shop for one, though, be careful to look for the best quality. It is also important to go for the highest dpi rating you can afford. If your scanner can't tell the difference between an "n" or an "r," it's going to be more trouble than it's worth. When you go to the computer store, take along a floppy disk and a newspaper classified page (the one with jobs for writers). Run the page through the scanner, copy it to the disk, and take it home to see how it looks on your own screen.

Many word processing specialists consider a scanner as basic to their business as graphics designers do to theirs. Shawn Teets, who wishes she had bought one right at the start, says, "I do a lot of manuals, and when I started out I had to retype every word. Now I just run it through the scanner and what used to be a typing job is now a much easier editing job."

MODEMS

Another peripheral you're going to need is a modem (an abbreviation of the technical term modulator-demodulator) to connect your business to the outside world via telephone lines. Most modems transmit data at 9,600 or 14,400 bits per second, which is called the baud rate. You'll see numbers as high as 57,600 bps, which means that the modem is capable of compressing the data you're sending so it takes less time to move it over a telephone line. Keep in mind, though, that the efficiency of your online service and the efficiency of your telephone line are going to have an effect on your modem's speed. And when you use your modem for faxing, it can only be as fast as the one that receives the information. And you should, by the way, have a separate phone line dedicated to it.

FAX MACHINES

Many modems allow faxes to be sent directly to your computer. But most of them won't receive a fax if the computer isn't turned on, so if you expect to get faxes in the middle of the night or on your day off, it's a good idea to put a fax machine on your shopping list, too. You can also use it to make copies of letters and other documents, if you don't care too much about quality. If you do, a copying machine should be on your shopping list as well.

You can, of course, save that expense for better days. There are more places to have copies made in most neighborhoods than there are barbershops. And, if you're copying long documents, it's probably cheaper to let the copy shop handle it than to eat into your own time.

PRINTING PAPERS

Desktop publishers are the printers for a lot of jobs they produce, and for that you're going to need a selection of printing papers that will help you make those jobs look good. What you stock depends on what you're selling, but you may not be able to find what you like at the local stationery store.

Because desktop publishing services have grown so fast, there are dozens of mail-order houses eager to serve you. Look for their advertisements in computer and graphics arts magazines. You'll find their catalogs filled with different kinds of papers and forms that can be run through a laser printer with great results. Many of them also sell sample kits that include examples of the kinds of things you'll be producing, from tri-fold brochures to letterheads and business cards. Some sell prepackaged sets of all the kinds of papers you probably need. Just be careful not to buy what you're not going to need. And as a general rule of thumb, you shouldn't tie up your money in inventory you won't use up in about three months. There's a lot more where that came from, and most suppliers offer overnight delivery.

If paper is something you haven't given much thought to, you can get a good basic background in paper selection with *Pocket Pal*, a booklet published by the International Paper Company. Your printer probably has copies, or write to the company at 77 West 45th Street, New York, NY 10036. It's free, probably because it is a priceless resource.

YOUR WORKPLACE

A good reason for not stocking more paper than you need right away is the space it takes up. Once you begin accumulating equipment and supplies, the next important question is: Where are you going to put all that stuff? For a lot of reasons, not the least of which is the cost of renting outside space, the answer probably is somewhere in your home.

About 60 percent of all desktop publishers work at home. Those that don't are divided among designers with elaborate digital studios and people who prefer (and can afford) keeping their business and professional lives separate. Sometimes the business has outgrown the house and sometimes the people involved have discovered that working at home doesn't work for them. Ellen Connor is among them. After two years of working at home, and loving every minute of it, she reached the conclusion that she was "losing a lot of business because people don't know where I am." She believes that having an office closer to her prospective customers will pay for itself. Kevin Edwards moved his office from the house to the garage because he found that his family life was intruding on his work.

But even if some desktop publishers find it suits them better to go out to a studio every day, setting up an office at home makes good sense, at least at the start, for most of them.

When you put together a home office, don't confuse your two lives. Your workspace may be under the same roof as your bed-and-breakfast nook, but you need to think of it as a completely different world. That's what the IRS expects you to do, and even if you've got files and papers and computer manuals strewn all over the house, it isn't going to cut it with them. It shouldn't with you, either. You will be working to make a living, but don't make the mistake of living with your work.

To paraphrase the sign over the salad bar, take all the space you need, but use the space you take, and not a square foot more. Don't let your work spill over into your living space. Don't leave letters near the front door if your office is at the back of the house. And those computer magazines belong near your desk and not on the coffee table. Be obsessive about it. Your new business will infiltrate your personal world if you're not.

It is important to have a separate telephone line for your business. That way you'll be sure it is always answered in a professional way and, probably more important, it will make it easier to keep business and personal calls separate in your tax records. You might also consider a third line for your fax machine and your Internet connection—it could prove to be a time-saving convenience.

Keep the business phone lines in the part of the house where you'll be doing business because that is where your records and logs ought to be. Apart from having one of the kids answering your business phone, one of the most unprofessional things you can do is to ask a client to hold the phone while you run from the kitchen to your office to look something up.

It goes without saying that you should be able to put your finger on a client's file without a long search when one calls. That means you need to keep your workspace organized. You might think that since your office is your private domain, neatness doesn't count. You may even have a sign there that says "a sloppy desk is the sign of a creative mind," but don't believe a word of it. Let your creativity show in your work, not on your desk.

That isn't to say that your office should look like you're expecting a photographer to drop by from a decorating magazine. But suppose a client calls unexpectedly to talk about a contract. Your mind is lost in the job you're working on, and you can't for the life of you put your hands on that piece of paper, but for the life of your business you'd better be able to. If your office isn't organized, you won't be either. And if you're not organized, you're not only going to waste time, but miss opportunities too.

GET ONLINE

One of the most difficult transitions people experience when they shift from working in an office to working alone at home is the interaction with other people for help and encouragement. Working in a home office can sometimes be the loneliest job in the world. But many desktop publishers have found a way around it by chatting online with other people in the same business. It isn't always just idle chat. It's a way to get fast and friendly help when the computer warns you that an error has occurred but doesn't tell you what the error is and what you might do about it.

Tony Fry is among the good Samaritans. He switched from traditional ways of designing and became a desktop publisher back in 1986 with a MacPlus, and by now, he says, "any disaster that can happen has happened to me." Nobody ever forgets a disaster, nor how they worked themselves out of it, and they usually don't mind sharing their experience online.

And there are other reasons why you should subscribe to an online service. According to *Publish* magazine's subscriber survey, more than 65 percent of them use the WorldWide Web as a business tool. Some use the Internet to find new programs and download upgrades for old ones, others rely on E-mail to receive copy and to send proofs to clients.

SOFTWARE

It's against the rules to rent, borrow, or steal software. Software are the programs that make your computer do what you want it to do. Even if it weren't forbidden to copy someone else's programs, it isn't a good idea. The technical support software developers provide to registered owners through their 800 numbers and the manuals you get when you buy it are worth their weight in gold. When you're on a deadline and a software glitch pops up unexpectedly, you'll be grateful for the help. But don't forget to fill out the registration forms that come with them, and keep the registration numbers handy—they're your passwords to the help lines.

You're going to have to buy several software programs, including one to deal with word processing and some that will let you handle graphics.

GRAPHICS PROGRAMS

There are three basic types of graphics programs you should consider, but before you buy versions of any of them, check to make sure the service bureaus and the printers you're dealing with can work with the files they produce.

Page layout programs such as QuarkXpress and PageMaker

let you create the basic format of a document and import text and graphic elements into it as necessary for newsletters and other such documents. Programs like these are what made desktop publishing possible by giving designers an option to old-fashioned pasteups and throwing in near-unlimited flexibility into the bargain.

Illustration programs, like FreeHand and Illustrator (also called PostScript drawing programs) help you produce original artwork in the form of printer-coded EPS files (Encapsulated PostScript) that allow a printer to deliver the highest possible resolution. They have revolutionized the business of designing things such as CD covers and product packages as well as brochures and direct-mail pieces. The output of an illustration program is often called "object-oriented," which means that what you draw is what you get when you make a printout. And it is always clearer, sharper, and smoother than what you see on the screen.

Image-editing programs, such as Photoshop and ClarisWorks, are sometimes called "painting programs." They produce what are known as "bitmapped" graphics, which is to say that the computer stores a graphic one pixel at a time as a sort of map of the screen. That is why they take up so much memory. A bitmap is a database of the number and color of each dot that makes up an image. The advantage is that you can retouch a photograph dot by dot, and even combine the elements of several of them to create something brand-new. They produce pixel-based TIFF files (Tagged Image File Format), which usually start out as the product of a scanner.

If you expect to do anything other than word processing, you should regard all three types as basic equipment. After you've gathered experience with them, you can go on from there with new programs that will make your work unique.

Be forewarned: graphics programs tend to be expensive and it takes time to learn them. They put a huge drain on your computer's memory, too, which means you may have to go to the expense of adding some more. If you are anxious to get started and your budget is limited, buy them one at a time, keeping in mind the kind of work you'll largely be doing. But plan to have all three types eventually and then there will be nothing you can't accomplish.

START LEARNING WITH A PROGRAM PACKAGE

Some software developers offer several desktop publishing programs bundled together, and at times they're even included with hardware packages. William Judd, who teaches computer basics at the Virginia Commonwealth University uses Microsoft Works in his classes as an introduction to desktop publishing "because," as he puts it, "it's a great combination of word processing and graphics." Once his students master Works, he finds that going on to more sophisticated programs is much easier for them. If you're planning to teach yourself how to manipulate a variety of software programs, Works could be a good place for you to get your feet wet.

Be wary, though, even though bundling can make starting out easier, some packages may include things you don't want or can't use, and there may not be a cost advantage in buying one. (Worse, bundled software may not come with the manuals or allow you access to technical support!) The computer business is like the toy business, and most of the things you need to make your business work are sold separately.

BECOME A STUDENT AGAIN

Learning a new program is like learning to ride a bicycle. It seems impossible at first, but once you get the hang of it, you wonder what all the fuss was about. It's also a bit like learning to cook. You can follow the instructions that come with it, like a cookbook, but the best way to learn is to have someone walk you through it.

It's the same with computer programs, and that means taking an instruction course. In most parts of the country, computer courses are offered through adult education programs, and you may even find them offered by computer dealers, but the best way to get training is through an accredited learning institution such as a college or university because that way you'll qualify for student discounts on equipment and software. The savings can be significant, and you don't have to be a full-time student to get them.

Many of Professor Judd's students are part-timers, schoolteachers trying to stay one step ahead of their students in computer literacy. "I recommend that they sign up for the course in September, so they'll have a student ID good for the whole year," he says. "That way, they have access to the college bookstore right through June." And are the savings worth it? That Microsoft Works program he recommends is available in the school's bookstore for a *quarter* of the regular price.

But learning computer programs is only one reason to become a student again. If your design experience is limited, you can enhance your skill by taking graphic arts courses. Your computer gives you the tools, but you will enhance your ability to use them effectively by learning the basics of good design.

WHAT ABOUT SERVICE BUREAUS?

No matter how much hardware and software you buy, and no matter how sophisticated it is, there are some pieces of equipment you won't need day in and day out and you probably couldn't afford them even if you did. They include items such as big drum scanners and large-format printers, and a whole list of other components that are needed to convert your computer's output to printing plates. If you do any graphics work at all, you'll be dealing with a service bureau sooner or later.

You probably won't find specific listings for service bureaus in the Yellow Pages, even though everyone in the desktop publishing business refers to them by that name. Yet you know they're out there and that you're probably going to need one. Where do you turn?

First, it will help if you understand exactly what a service bureau does. Simply put, service bureaus function as the middleman between desktop publishers and printers. Versatile as it is, your desktop computer can't always produce the kind of output a printer needs to deliver a high-quality job. Service bureaus have the sophisticated equipment it takes to enhance your output and bridge the gap between desktop publishers and printers. Among the things they provide are prepress services like high-resolution scans, matchprints, digital production, and film output.

Sometimes a printer will double as a service bureau, and a quality photo lab may fill the bill, too, but you'll generally find what you need listed in the classified telephone directory under "Computer Graphics" or "Desktop Publishing Services." You're going to find your competitors there, too, but this time around look for ads that offer "output" or "prepress" services. And pay careful attention to the range of services they say they can provide.

You won't need a service bureau all the time because the printer you outsource with more often than not will accept a disk with a hard copy and detailed instructions. But even if you don't plan to use one anytime soon, you should make it a point to call on a couple of them before you start acquiring software. Find out what media they require and what they won't accept. Compatibility is essential when you outsource your work to a service bureau or a printer. Richie Minor says that poor planning is one of the most common problems he deals with among the clients of his service bureau. "Files are the raw materials of my business, and the time it takes to fix them is a real liability. Of course, we charge extra to do it, but the time it takes can bump other clients out of the line and that could be a crisis for them. It seems everybody in this business is on a tight deadline."

Most important, when you're talking with service bureau operators for the first time, look for signs that they'll be forgiving (and helpful) if you make a mistake. Even the most experienced professionals get it wrong every once in a while, but a haughty sneer and exasperated sigh is that last thing you need when you're on a deadline.

TECHNICAL SUPPORT

Richie Minor has earned a reputation as a troubleshooter, and most service bureau operators like him are ready and willing to help when things go wrong. Generally they are computer experts, and because the equipment they use is far more complex than yours, any problems you might have may seem like child's play to them.

When you buy software, it's reasonable to assume that things are going to go wrong, especially at the beginning when you're not familiar with what your programs can do. Software developers are aware of that, and they offer support through toll-free telephone numbers. If you have registered your purchase with them, they will walk you through any problem, and probably solve it in minutes. Just be sure when you call that you have your registration number handy, that the phone you use is next to your computer, and that the computer is turned on.

Companies that make computers and peripherals also offer technical support through 800 numbers, and in some cases, their phone lines are open around the clock. Service varies, though, and with some programs you can get faster and more detailed attention by paying a fee for it. If not, you might want to reconsider your purchase. Most of the companies whose products you'll be using also have Web sites where you can turn for help when you need it. If you are considering buying bundled software, make sure that you will have access to the software manufacturer's technical support.

And if you're having an unexpected problem, chances are good that someone you have access to has already solved it. Many desktop publishers network with others who are using the same hardware and software and trade solutions with one another. Some do it in their own neighborhood, but most use their online service to reach other desktop publishers. Others also make it a point to get to know a technology maven—a computer teacher, a dealer, maybe even a savvy teenager.

Yes, things can go wrong when you're working with something as complex as a computer, but remember that you're not alone when a problem comes up.

CAN YOU GO IT ALONE?

A desktop publisher is like a one-man band, doing everything from drumming up business to taking the applause for a job well done. Most find hiring employees is out of the question at the beginning when they're struggling to pay themselves a salary. And even down the road, many shy away from the responsibility of meeting a payroll.

For some desktop publishers, there are times when freelancers need to be called in to handle overloads, but others make it a point to take on just enough work to keep them busy and avoid any surges they can't handle on their own. Susan Abbott, whose St. Paul, Minnesota, company, Abbott & Abbott, specializes in designing with type, is among them. "I don't use much outside help," she says. "I'm too picky and I usually wind up redoing the work anyway."

Chris Petrone, who worked for years with a staff of as many

as eight people mainly handling prepress work, decided to pare down and let service bureaus do the job for him. "There are a lot more service bureaus around here now than when I started out," he notes. "And I'd rather let them worry about the help and the equipment." He came to the decision the hard way, though. "One of the guys hit a wrong key and four megs of information vanished. We were able to recover it because making backups is imperative in this business. But my business came to a stop while we rebuilt those files, and I can't afford that."

Taking on extra help is a big financial consideration, but there may come a time when you'll need someone to help you turn a job around in a hurry. The best way to find freelance help is by networking, especially through professional organizations. Through previous jobs, you may have met people who can help you. Or you might look for ads in the local trade press or the Yellow Pages. Take care, though, to check out references, work samples, and, most of all, personalities. Remember, you're looking for help, not more problems.

But aside from a service bureau, a reliable printer and someone to take the load off once in a while, how much other kind of help will you need?

WILL YOU NEED A LAWYER?

Richie Minor works with two lawyers in his service bureau business, but he confesses that one of them is a friend "who enjoys sending out letters to people who have owed me money for too long." The other helped him set up his corporation, and still keeps an eye on it for him.

But the fact is, he doesn't call on either of them very often, except socially. And chances are good that you won't have to, either, especially if you're going to be operating out of your home and don't expect to have any full-time employees. That doesn't mean you won't need a lawyer at the beginning, though.

You need to protect yourself and your personal assets when you go into business for yourself. As one lawyer explains it, "if your business fails, you can lose your house, your car, and everything you own, including your computer equipment, unless you take the right steps before you start, and that includes setting up some form of a corporation to protect yourself."

Whether or not you keep an attorney at your beck and call through the life of your business, use one at the start to make sure you don't get off on the wrong foot. There are important things to consider like which form of business is best for you. There will be legal papers to file at the start, too. You'll be writing contracts with all kinds of clients, and you'll want to be sure all the bases are covered, including ways to avoid collection problems.

You also need a lawyer's advice in dealing with copyright law. As you go along, you may be working with words and images that might not be in public domain. If you alter a photograph or appropriate words from a song, for instance, you might find yourself hearing from someone else's lawyer.

Possibly the best place to find a lawyer is by calling the local Bar Association. In most places, they'll provide you with a list of attorneys in your area whose experience best suits your needs, and they'll give you some idea of what you can expect to pay. You can also ask other people with small businesses for recommendations, or your accountant who may know of a lawyer who will understand your particular business.

Legal fees vary from area to area and from lawyer to lawyer, and everything else being equal, it pays to do a little comparison shopping. You may find, as other desktop publishers have, that you only have to pay a reasonable flat fee for the paperwork you'll need. But you will pay by the hour for a consultation, and with that in mind, you ought to have some idea of what your options are before you sit down in a lawyer's office.

WHAT FORM SHOULD YOUR BUSINESS TAKE?

Some desktop publishers simply operate like freelancers without a day job. Their businesses are usually called sole proprietorships, but accountants often refer to them as Schedule C businesses, so named because of the federal income tax form they need to fill out. But the problem with a proprietorship is that your personal assets and your business assets get all mixed up, because as far as the tax people are concerned, your income from your business is no different than if you were earning a salary. It's the same with creditors. Your business debts are the same to them as your personal ones, and if your business gets into financial trouble, you might find your personal bank accounts frozen, and you can lose everything you own whether it has anything to do with your business or not. If you plan to keep your business small, you may think you won't have to worry about such things; but if you expect it to grow, and it undoubtedly will, you're going to need to find a way to separate business from pleasure.

Like most professions, desktop publishing is a highly personal business, and partnerships are relatively rare—but they do exist.

A legal partnership, like a sole proprietorship, makes no distinction between your personal and your business assets. And to make matters worse, you don't have the same amount of control over either one because you have a partner's input to contend with.

When you enter into a partnership, your liability isn't limited to your original investment, and if your partner drains the company dry—and it does happen, even among the best of friends—you will be responsible for every penny of its debts.

In the world of big business, investors form corporations and declare themselves shareholders. If the corporation goes bankrupt, they are not responsible for anything more than their original investment. But before you start issuing stock in your venture, you need to consider the downside. It's a big one. You'll owe the federal government a huge corporate tax on any profits you make, and many states also levy their own corporate tax on top of that. If you pay yourself any dividends, they have to be reported when you file your personal income tax return, and you'll find yourself paying tax on money that has already been taxed.

But for small businesses like desktop publishing, the IRS has come up with a different kind of structure it calls Subchapter S. It gives you the benefits of being incorporated but without most of the burdens. Basically, Subchapter S allows businesses and professional people to be considered a corporation, except when the time comes to pay the taxes. Subchapter S corporations don't pay corporate income taxes on their profits. Instead, their owners are taxed just once on April 15. They are allowed to deduct business losses and expenses, which can reduce personal income taxes, especially at the beginning when the business is reinvesting its profits in equipment. There are some restrictions in the Sub-chapter S scenario. They are limited to seventy-five investors, all of whom must be U.S. citizens, for instance.

There are even fewer limitations with a new kind of business form that has recently come on the scene—the limited liability company, which offers the limited liabilities of a corporation but is taxed like a partnership or a sole proprietorship. LLCs can have any number of investors, and these investors may be citizens of any country. Like a partnership, they have a predetermined life, usually thirty years, which can be extended. And in some states, but not all, they need to have the earmarks of a partner-ship with a requirement that at least two persons must form the company.

For a desktop publishing business, a limited liability company may well be the best way to go. The revised federal tax law of 1996 made Subchapter S corporations more like LLCs. There are still differences, though, and those that will affect you when you're starting up a new business are more likely to be on the local level. Some states don't recognize the Subchapter S concept, for instance, and they tax such companies as unincorporated businesses. Because there are so many variables, you absolutely must talk with your lawyer or your accountant about them before you make a decision—not only can this save you money every tax year, but it will protect your personal assets at the same time.

WILL YOU NEED AN ACCOUNTANT?

Shawn Teets has never used an accountant to help her run her company, but, then again, she's never used one to help her with her taxes either. Angela Haglund does her own bookkeeping too, but she says she wishes she had an accountant to help her.

Some desktop publishers use financial software on their computers to do the work of an accountant, but most say they prefer going to a professional. Susan Abbott is among them. She hired an accountant who set up her books for her and showed her how to keep them. She pays him a monthly fee, and he reviews her books every quarter and also helps with her taxes. She says she couldn't get along without the service, particularly because "the local sales tax is a gray area here in St. Paul. I have to collect it and pay it." It's one more time-consuming detail she'd rather not have to deal with.

AN ACCOUNTANT'S VIEW

Irwin Fenichel, a partner in the New York City accounting firm of Edward Isaacs & Compay LLP, says that most small businesses like desktop publishers use his firm's services for taxes, financial statements, and bookkeeping.

In his experience, most entrepreneurial types "have a careless attitude about money." He says that he finds that they have more faith in the future than they probably should, and don't usually care about going into debt because they believe they're going to hit it big one of these days. It may be a great outlook on life, but, as he puts it, "they need an accountant to rein them in a little."

When he works with a new small business start-up, his key consideration is capital and financing. In just about every kind of small business, there are long months at the beginning when there is no money coming in to take care of daily expenses, and he wants to be sure a new businessperson is able to deal with this, because there is often nowhere to turn for help. "Banks aren't very comfortable with new businesses," he warns, "and less so with service businesses."

When he studies a client's financial statements, the most important thing he looks for is debt to equity because "a heavily leveraged business has a serious problem." He also looks carefully at business plans and pays special attention to projections. "Banks do, too," he adds.

As for hiring an accountant, he advises that "it's a two-way street. Both parties need to be comfortable with one another, and I need to feel I can recommend a client to a bank or to an investor."

MONEY MATTERS

Without an accountant, you may have a hard time keeping up with all the information that is crucial to the life of your business—things like expenses and accounts receivable. Your accountant can help you determine how much cash flow you need to stay afloat, and blow the whistle when money isn't coming in fast enough. If you find that you need a loan to keep you going or to expand once you've established yourself, an accountant will put together the paperwork the lender wants to see, and not only give you advice about what sort of loan to ask for, but often where to take your application.

And when your business goes over the top, your accountant will be indispensable in handling all the details that go with adding employees—from payroll taxes to tax withholding. Then, when you begin making more money than you know what to do with, a good accountant will take care of your investment strategy as well.

ARE YOU INSURED FOR THAT?

Your lawyer can also be helpful in recommending the kinds of insurance you should have. You'll need protection against fire and theft, of course, and liability insurance. Most important of all, you'll certainly need a medical insurance policy, preferably one that will help you keep your business functioning if you need hospitalization. Remember that there is no such thing as a "sick day" when you're in business for yourself.

Many desktop publishers have medical insurance through working spouses. But they're the lucky ones. What if you're single or supporting a family on your own? Health insurance rates for individuals can sometimes seem as high as the mortgage on your house. And, like the house, you can't get along without it.

Being part of a group is one way to cut the expense. Your accountant may be able to help you find one, or you might try networking among other small business owners. In some areas, established business organizations or the local chamber of commerce offer health coverage at group rates.

You can also cut the expense of medical insurance by going for a high-deductible policy. The premiums are lower, but remember you'll pay more money to a doctor or a hospital when you use it.

When you announce that you are open for business, you can count on getting letters and phone calls from all sorts of people trying to sell you something, and medical insurance is high on the list, but be careful not to buy anything from anyone unless you have every reason to believe you're dealing with a reputable company, no matter how attractive the rate might seem. Remember the old rule that if it seems too good to be true, it probably is.

In the years ahead, your insurance needs will change as your business expands. You may want to offer medical coverage to your employees if you begin adding them, and you'll be expected to contribute to the worker's compensation plan. If your business grows to the point where you have a staff depending on it for their living, you may also want "key-person" coverage to keep it alive if you should die. And on the more positive side of life, you ought to have a pension plan, so you will be able to retire someday.

All of those items are available from a single source—a good insurance agent. Like travel agents, these people don't charge fees either for advice or for looking out for your changing needs. Their income is from commissions on the premiums you pay, year in and year out, so your insurance agent can be expected to be at your service as long as you're in business.

Be careful when you choose one. Look for an insurance agent who represents more than one company. Many do, and that gives you the advantage of comparing cost and coverage without going to several different sources. You'll also want an agent who is familiar with small businesses such as yours and can anticipate your needs. Chances are the person who sold you life insurance and your homeowner's policy may not be the one to take care of your business. It's a good idea to ask other business owners for recommendations, and also to meet with several agents before you have one draw up your policies.

CHAPTER SEVEN

Your First Customer

Before you start looking for clients, you need to know what you're going to charge. Be forewarned: this will present a thicket of variables that adds up to a nightmare for most desktop publishers. Ellen Connor, who is a desktop publishing chat room host on AOL, says that "what they should charge is by far the biggest question people have when they sign on." And she adds that seasoned pros wrestle with the problem almost as much as newcomers.

The store that sells you software has it easy. It has a suggested retail price set by the manufacturer. The manager knows what the store paid for the package, and how much the price can be cut to lure you in. But desktop publishers don't have simple guidelines like that when it comes to setting fees. You can't charge too much or you won't get any business, and if you charge too little you'll be out of business.

"It's the hardest thing there is," says Chris Petrone, "it's not like going to the supermarket and buying potatoes for forty-nine cents a pound." Like many desktop publishers, Chris doesn't have a standard fee, and he charges according to the value of the job to the client and the type of business involved. Clients of his—such as Kraft Foods—will use the sales promotion materials he creates for them on a national and even an international basis, but similar posters and folders for a chain of local banks won't be used beyond the borders of a single state. He takes such things into consideration, but when all is said and done, he usually sets his fees based on his client's guidelines and the parameters of the job itself.

WHAT'S THE GOING RATE?

Pricing generally depends on what the traffic will bear in your neighborhood. Finding out what the competition charges is a good place to start. Some desktop publishers have websites with rate structures out there for the whole world to see, but unless your local competitors are on the web or have printed price lists, it's a touchy business finding out what they charge because you already know the answer to the question "Does Macy's tell Gimbels?" Still, it's worth a try.

Some people turn themselves into comparison shoppers when they start up a desktop publishing business and call others in the area for quotes on hypothetical jobs. A trick like that may work some of the time, but remember that you aren't going to appreciate wasting time on calls like that once you've become established yourself.

Most desktop publishers are open and helpful, and some may not regard you as competition yet. Just be careful to ask for a price list and not a client list. And you should be aware of the level of skill and range of equipment they are working with. Both are important factors in what they charge, and what you should charge, too. If they aren't forthcoming, your printer or service bureau may be able to give you some ballpark figures on the range of desktop publishing fees in your area.

CONSIDER STANDARD GUIDELINES

You might also consider investing in a copy of the *Pricing Guide for Desktop Publishing Services*, and its companion, *Pricing Tables: Desktop Services*, both published by Brenner Information Group in San Diego, California (619 538-0093). The guide explains costs and shows you how to understand pricing and how to set rates no matter where you're doing business. The tables are broken down by region and give average fees from a database of over 200,000 price points.

Cindy Dyer uses the *Graphic Arts Guild Pricing and Ethical Guidelines* as a guide to setting prices, even though she notes that "the prices are much higher than I, or my higher-billing colleagues, can charge in this area. I don't really believe that anyone anywhere actually charges that much, but it's good to be able to show that you are below the market."

Alon Feder has used the same pricing guide (available in most art supply stores) with similar results. "I was contacted through a referral by a company that sells a very expensive software product," he says. "They needed a large display ad in addition to potential future work, and I told them my price for the design was $3,000 plus expenses and markups.

"They did some shopping around and got a quote for $1,800 and another for $2,000. I turned to the guide and saw the prices for work like that went from $10,000 to $30,000. I'd have been happy with just $3,000! I pulled the prices out of the book and faxed them to the client just to show them I was giving them an incredible deal. I inferred that they might be comparing apples to oranges by strictly basing their design decision on price. I pointed out that there were other factors to consider, like the quality of my work and the response rate of similar ads I'd done for other clients.

"In the end, I knocked my price down to $2,200 and got the job. The client is extremely happy with the work, and I expect to get more of it from them. If my designs increase their business, they are not going to balk at my prices increasing since they took a chance on me and I took a chance on them with that first job."

Alon's philosophy is one of the best you might follow as you deal with setting a fee for a new client. Sometimes it may be a good idea to take future business into account when you quote a price for a job. Think of it as a foot in the door.

LET THE CLIENT BE YOUR GUIDE

The last factor in your pricing survey is your potential customer, but that's probably the trickiest one of all to nail down. Ask anyone what they expect to pay for a service and the answer is sure to be "as little as possible." On the other hand, most businesses work with budgets, and if you get close enough to a prospect you might be able to find out how much has been budgeted for desktop publishing services on a particular job.

WHAT DO YOU NEED TO EARN?

Obviously, your business should be working with a budget too, and you ought to do a little pencil-pushing before you agree to *any* price. Thanks to that business plan you put together, you know what it's costing you to deliver the goods. You know how much you've spent on equipment and all the things it takes to keep your business running, from the electric bill to the grocery bill. Add it all up and this will give you a good idea of what you'll have to earn in a month to hold it all together.

You can plan on working a lot of overtime and giving up your weekends, but for all practical purposes, you have twenty working days in a month and, at eight hours a day, that adds up to one hundred and sixty hours. But remember that some of your time is going to be spent selling and delivering jobs, checking proofs at the printer, and keeping track of your business. It's reasonable to assume that such things will take up at least a quarter of your time, so that leaves you with one hundred and twenty hours a month to make money. Divide your costs by one hundred and twenty and you'll have a good idea what you should be charging for an hour of your time just to break even. But the whole idea of going into business for yourself is to make a profit. Most service businesses mark up this number, which they call "direct labor," by 50 to 100 percent. Obviously, so should you.

Sometimes you may have to settle for less, to be sure, especially when you're getting established. But make that basic hourly rate your goal, and it will take a lot of the guesswork out of the pricing dilemma.

CONSIDER THE VARIABLES

But while you're pushing that pencil, go a step further to factor in some of the variables all desktop publishers deal with. You'll have jobs that have to be changed after you thought they were finished. And you'll have clients who will take their own sweet time sending you a check (consider forty-five days an average). Every now and then, you'll even work for someone who won't pay you at all.

Don't forget, too, that there are seasonal cycles in desktop publishing, and there are going to be months when you won't have enough work to keep you busy for one hundred and twenty hours. And then you'll have some months when there aren't enough hours to get it all done, too. But don't count on the times when you have to burn the midnight oil to even things out. If you were working for somebody other than yourself, you'd expect to be paid extra for overtime, wouldn't you?

The hourly rate you establish for yourself will be the basis for what you'll be charging for most jobs, but the prices you quote ought to be for the completed job based on how long you think it's going to take you to finish it. According to one recent survey, the average hourly rate for a desktop publisher is forty-five dollars (that's *average*!; your rate may be higher or lower), and you may be dealing with clients who make a lot less than that in their jobs. Some of them will be envious of your freedom anyway, so be careful that you don't rub salt in the wound.

People who specialize in word processing usually charge by the page, and most ask for at least half of the amount due before they start the job. The balance is due on delivery, and more often than not people looking for résumés or manuscripts opt for paying the full amount all at once—up front.

Any price you quote is not so much for the job itself but the results it will bring, and you should make that your top priority when you sit down with a prospective client. Remember the old salesman's rule, "Sell the sizzle, not the steak."

DRAW UP A CONTRACT

Any price you quote is also etched in stone. If it takes you longer than you thought it would to get a job done, you can't go back and bump up the price. However, often the extra time comes from changes the client makes along the way, which is why it's a good idea to have a contract before you start—even a simple letter of agreement is better than nothing. The point is to get it in writing. If your agreement spells out what is required from the beginning and includes a clause that you expect to be paid for contingencies, you'll avoid some red ink on your financial statement, not to mention misunderstandings.

ASK YOURSELF THE RIGHT QUESTIONS

Mark Shapiro who has been in the desktop publishing business in Northern California since the 1980s, has seen his average hourly rate double for trade jobs from thirty dollars to sixty dollars since he started out, and his retail rate is twice as high. "I charge by the project because that way a client knows up-front what it is going to cost. But I bill by the hour if they request revisions.

"Before you quote a price, there are a few questions you need to ask yourself: Are your clients small businesses or large corporations? Are you working retail—that is, is it a one-time job—or wholesale, where you have repeat business? And what do your competitors charge?

"After taking those things into account, I recommend that you shouldn't be either the cheapest or the most expensive. Instead, make yourself the best value for your client's investment."

WHAT ABOUT CREDIT?

Not too many years ago, the question of credit almost never came up with small business people. If a tree fell on your house on a day when the bank was closed, you had to make a trip to the liquor store to get a check cashed because the guy who was coming to pick up the pieces expected cash on the barrelhead.

These days, of course, you'd go to the bank's cash machine. On the other hand, vendors such as the tree man often won't take a check and certainly not a credit card, but many such small businesses are willing to accept credit. Is this a good idea for your business?

If you're dealing with corporate clients, you are already giving them a kind of credit because many corporate comptrollers consider any account paid in ninety days the same as cash on delivery. Even though most will settle bills faster for those people who provide a service and not a commodity like towels for the executive washroom, they still won't put you in the same category as payroll or taxes and therefore you can expect to wait for your money. On the positive side, you can be fairly confident that you will be paid.

CREDIT CARDS

Many desktop publishers who specialize in word processing and deal with individuals find that their customers appreciate the option of using credit cards, and sometimes it can make the difference between getting a job or losing it to a competitor.

Your bank will charge you a fee for every credit card transaction you complete, as well as an annual fee for having the service, so you may want to establish a minimum amount before a charge can be processed. Remember, too, that every time someone hands you a card, you have to call the bank to verify it and sometimes the long wait can be stressful for both you and the client, but this is a lot better than taking a check from someone you don't know and having an even longer wait until the check clears. Once you've called in a credit card number and been given an authorization, your payment is guaranteed. You've shifted any bad debt problems to somebody else and improved your cash flow.

The latest thing on the plastic-for-money scene is debit cards. You still have to pay a fee when you accept one, but it works like an ATM card, taking money directly from the customer's bank account. If there isn't enough there to cover your bill, you'll know it before you start working.

MAKING IT WORK

Almost anybody is a potential customer for your desktop publishing business, from the family down the block that needs invitations for their daughter's wedding to multinational corporations that have seen the wisdom of "farming out" the production of their collateral materials. The challenge is finding a way to connect your service to their needs.

You've probably already given some thought as to where you're going to find business—maybe from a former employer or friends who have said they can use your help—and it may be more than enough to push you from the shore.

Having just one or two clients, though, no matter how big or how promising they are, can be like building a house on sand. As accountant Irwin Fenichel puts it, ". . . concentration of risk, a small customer base, is something banks take a very dim view of and any small business owner needs to avoid it like the plague."

Sometimes the offer of a large, steady account can seem like reason enough to quit your job and strike off on your own, but in every field, clients' needs change and no matter how much work you are getting now, you can lose the account without warning or it can be expanded beyond your capacity to handle it. You're then faced with a choice of giving the client up or climbing on a treadmill that you're not going to find rewarding even if the financial rewards are there. Meanwhile, you've been so busy keeping that one client satisfied that you haven't been developing other accounts, a scenario that could leave you high and dry—or locked into a situation that's less satisfying than the job you left in the first place. One of the reasons you're thinking of going off on your own is to find independence. Don't make the mistake of being dependent on one client, no matter how much business they can send your way.

And believe it or not, you can be too successful. Yes, you should hope for the best in this new business of yours, but plan to ease into your business slowly, no matter how tempting those initial jobs may seem. And don't make the mistake of trying to make it without a family of clients. Keep the family small at the beginning, but never stop planning for growth, so that you can move forward as soon as you feel able to handle it.

WALK, DON'T RUN

Possibly the best advice for starting any kind of business is not to land running but to start out walking. It is easy to be dazzled by dollar signs when you're getting started, but sometimes earning those dollars will be more work than you bargained for.

One of the keys to a successful new business is to build it a buck at a time. It is especially good advice when you start a desktop publishing business because it is more specialized than most and you'll always be learning as you go along, but if you're like most people considering a desktop publishing business, you've been working with computers and already know the basics. Maybe you've read every book and explored every desktop publishing site online and you're raring to go. In spite of all this, you should still move at a measured pace. At the very least, it will give you time to perfect your skills.

FINDING BUSINESS

Talk to a desktop publisher about where business leads come from, and the answer most often will be "word of mouth." And throughout the life of your business, satisfied clients are going to be your best source of new accounts.

When you're starting out, however, you'll need more than referrals. You'll need to get the word out to people who need your services but don't know you or don't know anyone you've ever worked with. To do that, you should develop a marketing plan—a road map to where your prospects are and the best routes to take to reach them. Marketing plans are second nature to large companies, and most of them regard them as matters of life and death. The same resources they use are also available to you.

The way professional marketers begin to find such prospects is by studying statistics, beginning with those they call demographics, which is simply where people live, how they make their living, and what their lifestyle is like. Such numbers, and names, that apply to your local business community are usually available at the nearest library or through the chamber of commerce or some similar business development organization. The numbers will give you a good idea of the potential of the market in your area and will help you get a better focus on areas of opportunity.

The second set of statistics big marketers treasure, called psychographics, gives clues about what makes people buy one product or service over another. Through surveys and focus groups, marketers get clues that help them come up with what the advertising community sometimes calls a "unique selling proposition," the plan that can set their products apart from the competition and also turn prospects into loyal customers.

Small business people don't have the resources to retain high-priced marketing consultants to help them arrive at such conclusions, but they don't need them, either. Because their business are small, they're in closer contact with their customers, and every meeting with one becomes a mini focus group. Keep your ears open when you meet with your clients, and you'll learn something more than just the details of the job at hand. Listen to enough of them and you'll know what you're doing right. Then lead with those strengths in the ads, the brochures, the mailing pieces, and all the other things that come out of your marketing plan aimed at building new business.

BUILDING A BRAND

Identifying potential clients is only half the battle when you put together a marketing plan. The other half, targeting and reaching them, may be even more important.

Making your service unique can make all the difference when a client has to decide whether to hire you or one of your competitors. Build an image for yourself and the client's decision will be easy, and eventually, it will become more important than what you charge. The bottom line may be important when a client makes a buying decision, but in the end what they're getting for their money is most important of all to them.

Keep in mind that even though your product is a printed document, what you are actually selling is what that document can do for the people who are paying you to produce it. People who come to you for a résumé want a new job, nothing more, nothing less. A restaurateur who hires you to design menus is looking for a way to impress his clientele, otherwise the bill of fare scrawled on a blackboard would do. An organization that wants a newsletter is looking for a way to keep its members informed, but it also needs a way to make them proud to belong. An ad, a package design, a direct-mail piece all have just one purpose: to attract attention and build sales for your client.

When Sue Karlin's company, Suka & Friends, began producing annual reports for nonprofit organizations, she found that her opportunities "just grew because these people all know each other." But she doesn't just rely on word of mouth. She advertises in journals she knows will reach the nonprofit community with such reminders as, "We help you help others," and "We're part of your good work," a unique selling proposition if ever there was one.

Sue also uses direct mail, but not to sell a specific service. She mails postcards to clients and prospects on a regular basis with cartoons or photographs doctored in Photoshop to offer wry commentaries on the business world and life in the big city. She gets a good response from them, but, better still, she finds them tacked to office bulletin boards when she makes sales calls. Even when she makes a cold call, the word has already preceded her that doing business with her company might be fun as well as rewarding.

But even if you don't advertise your service or send out mailings, everything you do is a reflection on your style. Something as simple and as basic as your business card and your stationery is part of your image. Right from the beginning it is important to know the image you should be projecting, and work to keep building it.

CREATE A PORTFOLIO

No matter where you get your sales leads, you're going to have to meet face to face with a potential client before you get the job. And you can't depend on a firm handshake, a wink, and a smile to get the job for you. You need to *show* a prospect what you can do. When you make a sales call, take along a selection of work you've produced, and make it as close as possible to what your prospect is looking for. If a car dealership is looking for a brochure selling its service department, show them one that could have been used to build used-car sales.

But what if (you have every right to ask) you've never tapped into the automotive field? What if, for that matter, this is your first sales call and you're hoping it will get you your first job?

Of course, you have to be honest about it, but until you have built a collection of specific samples to show a prospect, consider putting together some pieces that will show what you *can* do. Create items that not only show off your design skills but will also demonstrate what your computer can do with all those programs you bought for it.

Alon Feder, who has been building and rebuilding his portfolio for more than a dozen years, proved that such a made-up piece could be effective when he found himself faced with a prospect who wanted a special graphic created.

"I had nothing in my portfolio that was anything like what they were looking for," he recalls, "but I knew I could do it, and the client decided she'd give me a chance. She asked me to come back the next day with a pencil sketch of my idea for handling

the assignment. I ran back to my office and created a very involved mockup in Photoshop, took the file to the service bureau,
and outputted it on a Canon Fiery.

"I walked into the client's office with this full-color mockup
and her jaw about dropped. Needless to say, I was hired and I
got another great piece for my portfolio."

Your portfolio will grow as your business does, of course, and
the time will come when you can adjust it to the specific needs
of a prospect. But even if you aren't able to front-load it with
jobs for museums when you take it to an art gallery operator, be
sure your portfolio is timely. Go over it frequently to make sure
you're showcasing your best work. There is no need to show
everything you've done, just the pieces you think are outstanding
examples of what you can do. Remember, too, that you'll get
better at what you do as you go along, and chances are so will
the programs you use. So edit, continually. Besides, a prospective
client will want to know what you've done lately.

MAKE A BROCHURE FOR YOURSELF

You'll probably be producing brochures for many of your clients,
so wouldn't it seem like a good idea to make one for yourself
first? You should have a brochure to sell your business, especially
if that is one of the things you're going to tell your prospects
they ought to have. It will serve as a showcase of the things you
can do, and when you make a sales call, you can leave it behind
instead of your portfolio. Even better, you can mail your brochure a couple of days before you appear in person. It might
make a prospect anxious to meet you.

Chris Petrone developed a slide presentation to help sell his
business, but he eventually converted it into a CD-ROM to reach
more prospects by mail in less time with less fuss. Shawn Teets
put together a brochure before she started her business, and she

purposely kept it simple so that she could change it every few months to reflect her growth.

DESIGN A DISTINCTIVE LOGO

One of the major areas of desktop publishing service is designing logos, the symbols that define a business's identity, and the most important logo you'll ever design is your own. Include it on your letterheads and business cards and you will have taken the first step in building your brand.

While you're designing your logo, make sure it will be readable when it's reduced, because you're going to want to put it on every job you produce. Clients don't usually mind, if you ask them for permission, as long as it's small and doesn't interfere with their message. Think of it as signing your work, just as other craftsmen do.

IT MAY PAY TO ADVERTISE

When you're putting together your marketing plan, the advertising salespeople at local newspapers and magazines, radio and television stations are a prime source of information about the local business community. All of them have media kits—another service provided by desktop publishers—and they're filled with information about the people they reach. Much of it can be priceless in your quest to find people you should be reaching too. The information will also be valuable to you in planning your own advertising.

A good rule of thumb for most businesses is to allot about five percent of annual sales to advertising, and you should also. However, consider yourself lucky—the hardware store around the corner will have to hire you to design its ads, but you'll be able to save that part of the cost by doing it yourself.

ADVERTISE ON A SCHEDULE

By the end of your first year in business, you'll have a good feel for what its cycles are and you'll be able to plan your advertising schedule around them. But in the meantime, when you see a slowdown coming, head it off with a well-placed ad. A daily newspaper doesn't need a lot of lead time to run your ad, and neither do most local trade magazines.

Otherwise, it's a good idea to plan an advertising schedule paced to the needs of businesses you believe are your best targets. Corporate prospects might slow down in December when budgets are used up and everybody is in a holiday mood. Yet that is when the retail world is humming, and stores may be looking for printed material to keep the momentum going. At the end of the tax year, charities will be pushing for donations, and financial institutions promoting tax-free investments. In each instance, their own employees will probably be in a holiday mood, too, and they'll welcome some outside help. Just let them know how much help you can provide with a little extra advertising in the newspapers and journals those media kits have told you your prospective clients are likely to read.

PRINT ADVERTISING

Print advertising comes in two flavors—classified and display. You already know about classifieds if you've ever hunted for a job or for a place to live. Most newspapers and trade magazines have classified columns for business services, and you can run relatively low-cost display ads within them to reach people who are looking for your specific service.

Display ads can be anything from an inch deep and a column wide to a full page. Buy as much space as you think you need to get your message across, but, more than likely, anything bigger than a couple of column inches is a waste of money for a desktop publisher. But even small display ads will help separate you from the common herd, and they can attract customers who hadn't been thinking about a service like yours until your ad caught their eye—and of course it will, if you have your own eye on your image and have created the best-designed ad on the page.

Catching a potential customer's eye is the first rule of advertising, of course, and it is how you telegraph your own brand image. But the second rule may be even more important. It is often called the KISS rule: "Keep it simple, stupid." And keep in mind that your ad is just a door opener. The real selling doesn't begin until a prospect picks up the phone, so don't forget to return those calls. And no matter how frazzled you may be, do it with a smile in your voice.

KEEP IT LOCAL

Unless your services extend beyond your local area—into national markets for direct-mail packages or into cyberspace with web designs, for instance—you should concentrate your advertising where your client pool is, right around the corner. Karen Cunningham, who has made a specialty of typing manuscripts, decided to advertise in a trade magazine aimed at writers as a way of reaching more authors. But as a national publication, its advertising rates were far too high for a small business like hers. She reached a lot of people who could use a service like hers, but not enough who were near enough to her base in Louisville to become her clients. Although she ran a small ad in the magazine every month for a year, she vows, "I'd definitely not do that again at those prices." On the other hand, Karen says that the best business decision she ever made was running ads in the local Yellow Pages.

THE YELLOW PAGES

One place where you don't have to worry about timing your advertising is the classified telephone directory. When you run an ad there, it has a lifespan of a year, and you will be billed every month for the privilege. There is no way to scale it down in months when you can't handle the business. But you ought to be listed there, and you probably should consider running a display ad too.

Yellow Page advertising is especially important if you are specializing in word processing. Anyone looking for a résumé, for instance, will most likely look in the Yellow Pages first. And, as Karen Cunningham found out, the same is true of anyone who needs manuscripts or other papers produced.

Before you call to order your ad, take a close look at the directory you already have. Pick a heading that best reflects the service you plan to offer—graphic arts or desktop publishing services, résumés or typing services. Look on those pages to see how big the average display ads are so you'll have a better idea how large yours should be. As you'll notice, larger ads are generally placed closer to the top of the page. But you're a designer—even if you have a word processing business, your computer can help you develop outstanding designs. Make your ad better and it will stand out anywhere on the page.

If you plan to offer a variety of services, consider buying one-line listings in all the categories that apply, except the one you expect will attract the most business. For that heading run a display ad describing all the things you can do, and the other listings will carry a page reference to it.

Maybe you can't afford to be all that thorough at the beginning, and in the interest of saving money you might opt for running a single one-line listing. It may be all you need when you're starting up a new business anyway. You need to get off the ground slowly and don't want to put yourself in the position of soliciting business you aren't ready for. But whatever you do, make your presence known in the Yellow Pages. It's where a lot of potential clients will be looking for you.

TURN THE YELLOW PAGES INTO A PROFIT CENTER

The Yellow Pages, incidentally, can get you clients in a way you might not have imagined. When a small business orders a display ad, the phone company will offer to design it. That's why so much telephone directory advertising looks the same. Obviously, the people who put together the Yellow Pages aren't going to send their customers to you, but you can find them in the book, and offering to design next year's ad can be a foot in the door for bigger jobs—especially when the ad you designed helps your client get more business.

SELLING BY MAIL

While you're browsing through the classified telephone book, look for businesses you think might have a need for your desktop publishing services. Look under classifications like contractors or movers, restaurants or financial services, or whatever strikes your fancy. Be creative. Every business classification has a need for some kind of desktop publishing service, even if they don't know it yet. Every listing has an address, and all of those addresses add up to a mailing list.

Ellen Connor has made that central to her marketing plan and has found a lot of clients that way. She says that she picks a different business to target every month. "Last month it was travel agents," she says, "and I went through the Yellow Pages and sent a letter to every agent with a listing. I always get a good response, the mailings don't cost much, and it doesn't take much of my time."

Sure, a lot of your letters will get tossed out. Even among professional direct-mail experts who fine-tune their lists, the average response to unsolicited direct mail is anywhere from two to five percent, but Ellen's response rate is higher than that, in spite of her scatter-shot approach. If one or two give you a call, it may be worth the effort. Using your Yellow Pages list, your pitch can be specific and personal. And that makes it more likely to be read.

Among the prospects who respond, some are going to say, "Thanks, but no thanks," but that doesn't mean you've lost them forever. Save their names in your computer and keep in touch with them. Maybe you'll produce a job down the road that could be useful to their business. When you do, send them a copy with a short note saying that you thought they'd be interested. They very well might be.

WRITE YOUR OWN NEWSLETTER

Many people in the word processing business produce newsletters for their clients. Some also put together newsletters of their own, which they mail to both their clients and their prospects. It's a way of saying, "I'm still here and still ready to serve you." And it's a great way to show that you're thriving.

Clip articles from newspapers and magazines whenever you find one you think would interest your universe of clients. Then write your own summaries of them for your newsletter. It is well worth the effort when you're trolling for new accounts, but, more important, it also helps to remind your existing clients that you are interested in their business too.

It is one more way to showcase your brand, and to demonstrate what you can do with layouts and graphics. Be careful, though, articles that appear in newspapers and magazines are copyrighted. It's generally acceptable to include brief, credited, quotes, but never to reproduce whole articles without permission.

FREE ADVERTISING

One of these days, you're going to bump into a prospect on the street or in the checkout line at the supermarket. It will be an old friend or an acquaintance who knows you've gone into the desktop publishing business but has neglected to use your service. "I've been meaning to call you," they'll gush. Then you'll exchange business cards and you may wind up with a job you hadn't expected.

That person, by the way, might have called long ago if you had sent a letter to all those friends and acquaintances telling them about your new business. It doesn't have to be an out-and-out solicitation, but rather a subtle suggestion that you might be offering a service they can use.

But suppose you hadn't been on that street corner at that precise moment, or decided to put off the grocery shopping. Do you think they'd have called you? Probably not. There are no truer words than "out of sight, out of mind," but you can't be everywhere, and you can't expect to bump into business every time you decide to take a walk in the park. (However, don't ever leave home without a supply of your business cards.)

PRESS RELEASES

There are a few ways you can keep your name out there, even when your face is glued to the computer screen. One of them is to send out press releases to local papers as often as you can. You should do it when you start up, of course, but you could also create a general release on the field of desktop publishing and your part in it.

While the world of desktop publishing may seem quite familiar to you, it is new and fascinating to a lot of people who don't really know much about it. Describing what it is and how it works would make an interesting business page feature story. And think how much *more* interesting it would be if you were quoted in it from top to bottom.

As a desktop publisher, you might be, or will certainly become, an expert on computers and what they can do. Get to know reporters who cover technology and computers and encourage them to put your name on their Rolodexes for consulting (and quoting) on new developments. Once they get to know you, they'll call you. And they'll use your name in the stories they write. If you have a flair for writing yourself, you might even consider signing on to do a weekly column for your local paper. Offer to exchange it for advertising space.

USE BROADCASTERS

Broadcast personalities also manage to come up with "experts" to comment on the things they're reporting. There's no magic involved. Their producers keep files of contacts in every imaginable field, and when they need an expert, they just pick up the phone.

As an authority in a new field that changes as rapidly and dramatically as desktop publishing, there is no reason why your name shouldn't be in one of those files as well. But first you need to call the broadcaster's office and find the producer who will interview you. Once you've done that, you'll have to wait for your big break in the form of a telephone summons. That's show business.

GO FOR AWARDS

You should also make it a point to submit your work in every competition you can (or, even better, get your clients to do it for you). Advertising agencies thrive on the awards they've gathered. You know the routine, movie stars are often promoted as "nominated for an Academy Award," even if they've never won one.

Even an "honorable mention" can go a long way in advancing your prestige, and you don't have to enter national competitions to make a good impression. Recognition from the local chamber of commerce, a regional trade association, or the art directors' club is going to get your name in the papers—and it deserves a place in your portfolio.

HAUNT BULLETIN BOARDS

A more mundane but sometimes overlooked, no-cost way to keep your name in the public eye is with public bulletin boards. You know the ones, over there by the change machine at the Laundromat or in the supermarket vestibule. Some of your business is going to come from your neighbors who need business cards produced or want someone to type up that screenplay they've been working on all these years. You need to let them know that you're the person they're looking for.

Be careful to make your message more specific than "desktop publishing services." Not everyone will understand what that means. The woman offering yoga classes in the neighborhood probably doesn't realize that she's going to need a desktop publisher to produce the flyers and mailing pieces that will help her find students.

If your desktop publishing business will be offering secretarial services or word processing, haunt the bulletin boards at local colleges, hospitals, and government offices. In fact, there isn't a public message center you shouldn't consider. If people see your name in enough places, they'll begin to think they know you. And that is the best result you can expect from *any* kind of advertising.

SELL YOURSELF

Everybody knows that a customer who is pleased with your work will be a repeat customer. But keeping a client satisfied goes beyond delivering a dynamite job. As the old song says, "It Ain't What You Do, It's The Way That You Do It."

The most important thing you can do is make your clients feel important. That may seem too obvious to mention, but the business world is a lot less personal today than it once was. In many places, old-fashioned courtesy seems to have become just that: an old-fashioned idea. But you can easily turn that into an advantage. In a world where there is so little of it, simple courtesy can stand out like a summer sunrise. It doesn't take any effort, and it doesn't cost a thing—just a simple "thank you" for the business can work wonders.

A friendly attitude can go a long way with everyone you deal with. If the people who run printing presses for you are partial to jelly doughnuts, take along a bagful of them when you go there. It will get their attention, and may even get you a better job.

When you visit a client's office, don't rush past the receptionist without stopping to chat for a minute or so. The gesture will be remembered when the time comes that you have to interrupt a client's meeting for a phone call that can't wait.

The fact is, everybody in an office you visit is as important as the person you've gone there to see. For one thing, some of those people are going to be promoted one of these days, and others are going to move on to different companies. Make sure they'll all remember you.

LEAVE-BEHINDS

Friendliness is free, but some people in service businesses take it a step further by leaving gifts behind to help people remember their names. It doesn't have to be expensive. Most companies frown on expensive gifts, anyway. But something like an inscribed marking pen or a notepad, a poster you've created with an interesting graphic or a humorous postcard like the ones Sue Karlin finds so effective, can be worth a lot more than the pennies they will cost you. You'll find sources for some of those things under "Advertising Specialties" in the Yellow Pages. Just be sure that the things you leave behind reflect the image you've developed for yourself. You're looking for a whole lot more than a handy reminder of your name and address.

You may also find clients among those ad specialty sources. Every imprint they sell needs art prepared for it. You might even consider bartering the service for the premiums you want for yourself.

NETWORK YOUR WAY TO NEW BUSINESS

Establishing a network simply means keeping in touch with old friends and associates as often as you can. It also means making contacts by meeting new people face to face whenever possible. No one will approach a stranger when they actually know someone who can help them solve a problem.

Even if some of the people you meet may never need the services of a desktop publisher, it's a good bet they'll be your best promoter among their friends who might. People take great pleasure in recommending sources to their friends. "Hey, I know someone who can help you!" is one of the friendliest statements there is because it connects friends who might otherwise have been strangers. And sometimes it can be surprising where big, profitable jobs come from.

DEVELOP CENTERS OF INFLUENCE

At some point in your life, maybe when you got married or promoted in your job, you probably had a call from a life insurance agent. When you finally agreed to listen to the sales pitch, you may have discovered that your best friend put him on to you. Then, as you signed on the dotted line, he asked you if you had any other friends who might need coverage. Of course you did, and the agent had some new leads. That technique, called "centers of influence," has sold billions of dollars' worth of life insurance over the years, and it still works. It's another form of networking.

It can work wonders for you too. If a client praises your work, don't be a shrinking violet. Ask for a letter that you can put into your portfolio. Then ask for the name of someone else who should know what you can do. Either one might get you your next job.

People in today's business world are likely to have worked for several different companies before landing at the desk where you caught up with them. They often know people with needs similar to theirs, and they don't usually mind sharing sources with them. As you get to know your clients, you'll get a feel for who might be forthcoming and who might be put off. Chances are, though, you're going to find more of the former than the latter.

BE A JOINER

Over most of the country's history, professional salespeople measured their success by the number of organizations they belonged to. They may not have called it networking, but they all regarded it as the best way to make customers out of strangers.

Not everyone in the desktop publishing business agrees that membership in organizations can be a useful networking tool these days. Ellen Connor found that her local chamber of commerce was just interested in big businesses in the area and turned a cold shoulder to small ones like hers. Mark Robinson has no patience with the business organizations in his area either. "They just tend to solidify stereotypes," he says.

Others, on the other hand, do find benefits from being a joiner. Susan Abbott belongs to several organizations in her area, "because it is an expression of support for my clients who are active in them." She gets business that way too, but more often than not it is new assignments from old clients. Sue Karlin also belongs to several organizations, which she finds both "supportive and a good place to network." Tony Fry has found that belonging to a local association of creative people is a great networking opportunity too, not for new business, but as a source of freelance help when he needs it, and for trouble-shooting when his systems are giving him problems.

In the end, whether you become a joiner or not depends on the kinds of organizations in your neighborhood, your own personality, and the type of business you've decided to target. For many, it makes sense to join organizations like local business groups that are likely to have potential clients in their membership and service clubs, such as Lions and Kiwanis, whose members are usually business and professional people.

You'll also meet people, and make some good contacts, by joining sales and marketing groups and by signing up for seminars. Not only that, but you'll probably learn a thing or two in the bargain.

TRY VOLUNTEERING

Another thing you might consider is volunteering some time at institutions like the Y, the library, or the Red Cross. This will instantly connect you with others from your community and you might be pleasantly surprised at who *else* is volunteering.

Be leery, though, about volunteering too much of your desktop publishing service. It's a perfect way to showcase the things you can do, of course, and to produce samples for your portfolio that will impress clients. But it's possible to carry altruism too far, and you may find yourself spending more time than you intended producing work that you're not going to be paid for.

Keep in mind that some people will think that because you are at home most of the time playing around with a computer that you are either retired or independently wealthy. The business of desktop publishing is such a new concept that most people don't usually realize that someone like you is making a living from it.

KEEP UP WITH YOUR FIELD

When all is said and done and you are making a decent living as a desktop publisher, you'll still need to keep *up to the minute* on your own business in one of the fastest-changing fields on earth. Bookstores have whole sections devoted to computer software, but when you begin browsing through them, check the copyright dates and always go for the ones that are most current. There are a host of computer-related magazines and newspapers that will keep you informed on the newest software and will offer tips to help you get more out of the ones you are using. Many of them are also available online, some with daily updates to help you stay ahead of the pack.

Remember that as a desktop publisher you are in the information business, and the best way to succeed is to keep yourself informed. It's what your competition will be doing. And it's what your clients will expect. And it's what you will need to do to survive in a field that is changing as quickly as yours.

CHAPTER EIGHT

Do I Have a Business?

Once the start-up phase of your desktop publishing business and its day-to-day operation has become routine, step back and take a look at how your life has changed. Taking inventory is crucial to seeing what works, what doesn't, and how you might do things differently to improve your new life. Sometimes the most obvious things can be difficult to see when you're racing toward a deadline.

AM I FINDING THE SATISFACTION I HOPED FOR?

Be forewarned: satisfaction can be elusive at the start of any new business. There are few that don't experience hardship, particularly at the beginning, so consider it part of the package of your new venture.

It may be possible to become disenchanted because you are overwhelmed with work and don't see any end to it. If so, try to shift your focus and find work that is less time intensive or if it is economically feasible, consider lightening your load.

You might find yourself beginning to resent spending every waking hour working, even if you do enjoy the work. Fellow desktop publisher Cindy Dyer recommends scheduling small vacations every now and then. R&R is the secret ingredient that allows her to enjoy a work schedule that many people would consider punishing.

If procrastination leads to a backlog of work, consider scheduling your more tiresome jobs at a specific time early in the day to get them out of the way. It will give you a chance to look forward to the work that you have the rest of the afternoon.

But if too much work is not the problem and you find you're sitting around waiting for the phone to ring, review your marketing plan. Ask yourself if you've created a brand that appeals to your customer base, and, if so, are you selling it effectively? Are you visible enough, and, if not, what is the best way to network within your target market? Is that target market already oversaturated with desktop publishers? If this is the case, is there a niche out there that you have overlooked?

And look at the competition. If the competition is thriving, what's their secret? Are your prices too high? Are you offering a quality of work that can stand up to the competition?

As you go along, you'll find there are things you are doing that are unprofitable. Or work that you shouldn't have taken on . . . or a course that you never took that you really need. Mistakes are inevitable, but invaluable to you as you learn your trade.

You've come a long way in this business of yours, so if things don't seem to be working right, fight hard to come up with some creative answers. Remember, tiny adjustments can have a positive impact on your small business. And never hesitate to take your problems to the SCORE office, your accountant, or a small business consultant. It's worth the minimal fee.

AM I MAKING OR LOSING MONEY?

Sometimes the question isn't whether you're making or losing money, but when are those checks going to arrive? Just about every small business has cash-flow problems at one time or another, and desktop publishers certainly aren't immune to it. After you've been running your business for awhile, you may notice that bill collecting is a big part of it, even if it wasn't in your original job description.

Fortunately, many desktop publishers don't have collection problems. Karen Cunningham is among them. "I am very careful about who gets extended credit," she says, "and I usually get cash or a check before I deliver a job. If it is a long-distance account, I send it COD via mail or UPS." Yet, she adds that it was close to three years before "I could honestly say I was earning a living."

But not every desktop publisher has the luxury of up-front payments. Chris Petrone's bigger corporate clients take sixty to ninety days to pay for his work, and the clock doesn't start until the job is delivered. In his case, it took three years "to start paying myself a salary," and cash flow is still a problem after more than nine years in business. He has begun asking for payment in thirds—at the start, the middle, and the end of a job. Some of his clients balk at the idea, but a focus on shortening the times between payments was critical for him to improve cash flow.

Knowing whether you're making or losing money isn't always easy in a business like desktop publishing because the biggest commodity you're dealing with is time, and that doesn't lend itself to a balance sheet. But there are cash outlays that can get out of hand if you're not careful.

Many graphic designers who have become desktop publishers started out working at a drawing board, and although art supplies were expensive, keeping track of costs was fairly simple. Switching to computers has not only proved to be much more expensive but also much harder to control. If you're not careful, before you know it, you could drown in debt from things like RAM, extra phone lines, syquests, zips, toner, software, upgrades, and a host of other costs that didn't exist back in the old days. And it is often difficult to figure these out-of-pocket expenses when you set your fees.

If dealing with the financial aspect of your business is not one of your strengths, don't blunder along praying that you have enough money to cover your expenses. Hire an accountant! Schedule regular meetings and have your accountant tell you what he or she sees. Desktop publishing is your specialty, managing finances is the accountant's. Never underestimate how quickly small financial problems can snowball in a small business. Working with a financial expert will help you develop a better sense of your entire business.

IS IT TIME TO MODIFY MY ORIGINAL PLAN?

If, after time, you find that your business isn't producing as much income, or as much gratification as you had hoped for, the solution may be to use your skills and your equipment in another area of desktop publishing.

After several years of putting together provider directories for a managed care organization in Texas, Laurie Piper went into her own business creating newsletters for a half-dozen different clients. The business was a big success, and she was pleased with the variety that had been missing in her job. But along the way she discovered that she had a knack for, and an interest in, parenting. After researching the possibility of producing her own newsletter on raising children, she switched the emphasis of her business and began writing and marketing an eight-page newsletter that she distributes through school systems to parents of elementary-age children. "It takes up all my time," she says, and except for an occasional brochure for one of her old clients, the bulk of the work she is doing these days is for her own enterprise.

By changing her specialty, Laurie became a desktop publisher in the truest sense of the word, researching, writing, designing, producing, and marketing a product she found could fill a need. Many others like her have found that moving from one aspect of the desktop publishing business to another is not as daunting as it may seem.

Some who originally started a business providing word processing services have added graphic design to their specialties. And they often find that their new skills open new doors for them. Before taking that step, you'll surely need to take courses to develop those skills. And you'll have to invest in the software that will put them to work for you in the most effective way. If you think it will pay off in terms of satisfaction, happiness, or income, it may be a leap worth taking, just as the decision to start your own business was in the first place.

IS THIS THE LIFE FOR ME?

After three years as an independent desktop publisher, Kevin Edwards decided to go back to work for a printing company. "I used to work sixty hours a week," he recalls, "but only half of those hours were billable. I'm working forty now and making more money."

Was going out on his own a mistake? Not at all. In fact, he says, "I'd be kicking myself for the rest of my life if I hadn't done it."

Kevin loved the work, and he's still doing it as a freelancer, but he wasn't happy with the demands of the business itself. If he had it to do over again, he thinks he might have looked for a partner who could have taken care of the administrative details. "You're limited by what you can physically produce in this business," he says. "And I wasn't at all happy during the time I had to spend away from production—picking up work, delivery, phone service, invoicing, administrative paperwork, and dealing with cash-flow problems."

Then there was the problem of where he worked. Kevin originally set up shop in a spare room in his house, but it wasn't long before he found that the arrangement was costing him too much time. His kids, at age two and five, were happy to have him at home most of the day, but they didn't understand that he had work to do there. Eventually, he decided the only way to avoid the interruptions was to move his business into his garage. "The expense was worth it to have my own space," he says, "but it only took them three months to find me. You'd have to be heartless to turn away a two-year-old, but it was just too much of an interference in my business. Considering the financial problems I was having, the best solution for me was to find a 'real' job."

An unusual case? Possibly. It took as much courage for Kevin to close his business as it did to start it. No matter how promising a business may seem at the beginning, you may find after time that it's a better idea to cut your losses.

DO I SEE A BRIGHT FUTURE?

If you are disappointed with the progress or direction of your new business, analyze the possibilities of making the future brighter. It took a lot of courage to start up your own business in the first place, and the same things that kept you going then can help you turn it in the right direction.

No business enterprise is a sure thing, but thousands have discovered that the field of desktop publishing is filled with opportunities. There are potholes along the way, to be sure, but with foresight most of the deep ones can be avoided.

An eye on the future will help you secure the future of your business. If a major client suddenly goes under, hopefully you've been cultivating other options along the way. If you foresee competition mushrooming all around you, be ready to alter your plan by lowering your prices or developing a new specialty.

YOU'RE IN DISTINGUISHED COMPANY

Although it is one of the newest opportunities in the business world, as a desktop publisher you're going to be part of a centuries-old tradition. You'll be following in the footsteps of the old craftsmen who designed furniture, carved mantelpieces, created designs in silver or, yes, even designed magnificent books. The tools are certainly different today, but even medieval artisans relied on the tools at hand to transform their thoughts into something that was both beautiful and useful.

Desktop publishing is a world exploding with new possibilities. It is a world that didn't exist thirty years ago, and isn't the same as it was three months ago. There is always something new to learn, and a multitude of new directions your business can take. Whether you're turning out multicolor brochures or building elaborate sales kits, producing résumés, manuscripts, or even letters from Santa Claus, a little bit of your own personality goes into every job you produce.

If you're like most people who have found a second life in desktop publishing, you're going to find yourself looking back someday and asking yourself, "Why didn't I do this sooner?"